THE SCIENCE OF LEARNING PHYSICS
Cognitive Strategies for Improving Instruction

THE SCIENCE OF LEARNING PHYSICS
Cognitive Strategies for Improving Instruction

José P. Mestre
University of Illinois at Urbana-Champaign, USA

Jennifer L. Docktor
University of Wisconsin-La Crosse, USA

NEW JERSEY · LONDON · SINGAPORE · BEIJING · SHANGHAI · HONG KONG · TAIPEI · CHENNAI · TOKYO

Published by

World Scientific Publishing Co. Pte. Ltd.
5 Toh Tuck Link, Singapore 596224
USA office: 27 Warren Street, Suite 401-402, Hackensack, NJ 07601
UK office: 57 Shelton Street, Covent Garden, London WC2H 9HE

Library of Congress Cataloging-in-Publication Data
Names: Mestre, Jose P., author. | Docktor, Jennifer L., author.
Title: The science of learning physics : cognitive strategies for improving instruction /
   José P. Mestre, University of Illinois at Urbana-Champaign, USA,
   Jennifer L. Docktor, University of Wisconsin-La Crosse, USA.
Description: New Jersey : World Scientific, 2021. | Includes bibliographical references and index.
Identifiers: LCCN 2020042831 | ISBN 9789811226540 (hardcover) |
   ISBN 9789811227769 (paperback) | ISBN 9789811226557 (ebook) |
   ISBN 9789811226564 (mobi)
Subjects: LCSH: Physics--Study and teaching. | Cognition--Mathematical models.
Classification: LCC QC30 .M365 2020 | DDC 530.071/1--dc23
LC record available at https://lccn.loc.gov/2020042831

British Library Cataloguing-in-Publication Data
A catalogue record for this book is available from the British Library.

Copyright © 2021 by World Scientific Publishing Co. Pte. Ltd.

All rights reserved. This book, or parts thereof, may not be reproduced in any form or by any means, electronic or mechanical, including photocopying, recording or any information storage and retrieval system now known or to be invented, without written permission from the publisher.

For photocopying of material in this volume, please pay a copying fee through the Copyright Clearance Center, Inc., 222 Rosewood Drive, Danvers, MA 01923, USA. In this case permission to photocopy is not required from the publisher.

For any available supplementary material, please visit
https://www.worldscientific.com/worldscibooks/10.1142/11998#t=suppl

Printed in Singapore

Contents

Chapter 1: Introduction   1
1.1. What is this book about?   1
1.2. Why is this book needed?   2
1.3. What does it mean to teach better?   4
1.4. What are some contributing factors leading to many students finding physics difficult to learn?   5
1.5. What view undergirds this entire book?   6
1.6. How are the subsequent chapters of this book organized?   7
Reference   9

Chapter 2: The Formation of Concepts and How to Fix Broken Ones   11
2.1. What does research on students' concept formation tell us?   11
   2.1.1. A comparison of behaviorist and constructivist views of learning   11
   2.1.2. Conceptual difficulties in physics   14
   2.1.3. Example: A study with balls and tracks   17
2.2. What are the implications of research on students' concept formation for instruction?   22
2.3. Examples of teaching interventions based on learning research   25
References   34

Chapter 3: How Learning Looks for a Novice: Implications of Expert–Novice Research for Physics Teaching and Learning   37
3.1. What does expert–novice research tell us?   37
   3.1.1. Broad observations about novices and experts in physics   38

3.1.2. Some important expert–novice differences ... 40
3.1.3. Differences in what novices and experts notice when "doing" physics ... 41
3.1.4. Problem solving differences between novices and experts in physics ... 45
3.1.5. Can instruction be designed to promote expert-like behavior in physics? ... 46
    3.1.5.1. Short-term interventions ... 46
    3.1.5.2. Longer-term interventions ... 55
3.2. What are the implications of expert–novice research for instruction? ... 63
3.3. Examples of teaching interventions based on learning research ... 65
References ... 78

Chapter 4: From Manipulating Equations to a More Conceptual Approach: ... 83
How to Improve Problem Solving
4.1. What does research on problem solving tell us? ... 83
    4.1.1. Research on problem solving skills and approaches ... 83
    4.1.2. Problem representation is important ... 86
    4.1.3. Problem solving frameworks ... 91
    4.1.4. Assessment of problem solving ... 95
4.2. What are the implications of research on problem solving for instruction? ... 100
4.3. Examples of teaching interventions based on learning research ... 102
References ... 104

Chapter 5: Active Learning Strategies: ... 111
Engaging Students in their Own Learning is the Key to Learning
5.1. What does the research tell us? ... 111

5.1.1. Introduction and background	111
5.1.2. Reforming the "traditional" lecture classroom	116
5.1.3. Reforming the traditional laboratory or recitation experience	120
5.1.4. Reforming the "out-of-class" experience	123
5.1.5. Barriers to active learning instruction	125
5.1.6. The use of Communities of Practice to encourage reformed instruction	127
5.2. What are the implications of research on active learning for instruction?	129
5.3. Examples of teaching interventions based on learning research	131
References	133

Chapter 6: Students' Perceptions of Learning and their Study Habits — 141

6.1. What does research on students' perceptions of learning and studying tell us?	141
6.1.1. Research on study strategies	142
6.1.2. What are the actual patterns of learning and forgetting?	149
6.1.3. Students' metacognition about studying and learning	152
6.2. What are the implications of research into students' view of learning and studying for instruction?	156
6.3. Examples of teaching interventions based on learning research	158
References	162

Chapter 7: Testing in the Service of Learning: The Testing Effect and How it Promotes Long-Term Retention — 169

7.1. What does research on the "testing effect" tell us?	169
7.1.1. What is the testing effect?	170

7.1.2. Experimental findings on the testing effect 171
7.1.3. Relevance of the testing effect for physics instruction 173
7.1.4. Mechanisms leading to long-term retention from the testing effect 176
7.2. What are the implications of the testing effect for instruction? 178
7.3. Examples of teaching interventions based on learning research 179
References 182

Chapter 8: Concluding Remarks **185**
Reference 187

Index **189**

About the Authors **201**

Chapter
1 Introduction

1.1. What is this book about?

This book is about teaching and learning physics. It is intended for use by college-level instructors of physics, although high school instructors might also find it very useful. It targets undergraduate instruction with an emphasis on introductory physics, which is where most students taking physics are enrolled. However, the ideas in this book can also be used to improve teaching and learning in both upper-division undergraduate physics courses as well as graduate courses. Whether you are new to teaching physics or a seasoned veteran, we present a variety of ideas and strategies for you to consider. Some ideas might be a small "tweak" to your existing practices whereas others require more substantial revisions to instruction.

The discussions of student learning herein are based on research evidence accumulated over decades from various fields, including cognitive psychology, educational psychology, the learning sciences, and discipline-based education research including physics education research. Likewise, the teaching suggestions are also based on research findings. As for any other scientific endeavor, physics education research is an empirical field where experiments are performed (in the messy environment of classrooms, or in the lab where student behaviors can be explored under more controlled settings), data are analyzed and conclusions are drawn. Evidence from such research is then used to inform physics teaching and learning.

1.2. Why is this book needed?

There are three main reasons for why a book like this is needed:

1. **Advances in knowledge about teaching and learning.** There is a substantial body of knowledge about how people learn and how to make learning more efficient/effective. Although applications of this knowledge are finding their way into physics classrooms, much of the research on student learning remains unknown by physicists, or perhaps worse, unheeded by them. We aim to highlight many salient findings about teaching and learning, discuss their instructional implications, and provide teaching examples of how to apply them. Currently there are no resources like this for physics instructors; existing books on physics teaching are either sorely outdated or narrower in scope.
2. **Physics is leading the way in reforming undergraduate STEM (Science, Technology, Engineering and Mathematics) instruction.** Anyone who has taught physics quickly realizes that the concepts and problem solving techniques that form the backbone of physics instruction are difficult to learn by large numbers of students. Perhaps because they like solving difficult problems, physicists have viewed difficulties in learning physics as a challenging problem to be solved, and for many years, physicists have engaged in studying ways to make physics learning more tractable to larger numbers of students. Many examples exist of how this research has made its way to classrooms,

among the more notable ones is implementing active learning in large classes using classroom polling technologies (with "clickers").
3. **The way Ph.D. training is structured.** Ph.D. training in just about every field except for education, where pedagogy is emphasized, consists of learning the field broadly through course work and by conducting research deeply in a specific subfield and writing a dissertation. Ph.D. programs produce experts in content knowledge and neophytes in knowledge about teaching and learning. With rare exceptions, the courses taken en route to a Ph.D. are only in the discipline in question (in our case, physics). The Ph.D.s in physics who eventually become professors and teach physics are highly likely never to have taken a course on how students learn, or on the use of *evidence-based instructional practices* (EBIPs) to teach physics. Like learning any new endeavor, learning to use any of the many EBIPs available takes time and effort, and professors at all levels have pressures on their time. The result is that most take the path of least resistance in teaching and do what was done unto them—they lecture to students. Some people can learn well with the lecture method (most of us who become Ph.D. physicists, for example), probably not because they learn everything the first pass through by listening to a lecture, but because they are disciplined and work hard at learning the material outside of lectures. As someone teaching physics you may have spent countless hours solving problems and thinking about the subject matter on your own or by learning through interactions with fellow students or professors. As we will discuss later, more students will learn more physics with EBIP-based instruction, if they would only

be used. Two important conclusions to be drawn from the structure of Ph.D. programs are: (1) Upon graduation, the newly-minted Ph.D. is ready for additional "education" on how students learn and how to implement EBIPs, and (2) If the newly-minted Ph.D. teaches only using lectures, fewer students will learn and many capable students will drop out of science entirely (Tobias, 1990). In addition, someone teaching in the K-12 realm or at a teaching-focused institution might be *expected* to engage in innovative teaching practices without much training on how to do so.

1.3. What does it mean to teach better?

In higher education, it is a common practice to measure the quality of teaching by using teaching evaluations, which are almost entirely based on the opinions of those students receiving the instruction. Even if you get observed by a colleague, their evaluation might be focused on surface-level characteristics such as whether your presentation of material was sufficiently "polished." If the goal of teaching is to have students learn, it is strange that we do not use assessments of student learning as the measure of quality teaching. If an instructor has a modest degree of charisma, shows some degree of sympathy toward students, and is clear in the lecture delivery, he/she is practically guaranteed high teaching evaluations. However, sitting in a lecture and enjoying "the show" is no different than going to the movies and enjoying the show. Enjoying a lecture and being able to follow it develops familiarity with the subject covered, and often a false sense of competence, rather than actual competence. In fact, we will present evidence later that indicates that typical student study habits (e.g., reviewing notes and homework solutions) do not provide evidence that she or he can actually apply concepts to solve problems—attempting to solve problems is the way of gaining competence in problem solving. One does not train to run a marathon by watching videos of marathon runners.

1.4. What are some contributing factors leading to many students finding physics difficult to learn?

Physics instructors are very adept at explaining the concepts and problem solving procedures needed to succeed in introductory undergraduate physics courses. Therefore, it is often not obvious to physics instructors why exactly learning physics is difficult for many. We mention two important factors at play here. The first is referred to as "the expert's blind spot," meaning that once we know something at a deep level (physics in our case), it is difficult to put ourselves in the shoes of a novice to determine which are the ideas that are not obvious and why. For example, when faced with a physics problem, our students might tell us that they do not even know where to start, whereas we have seen so many similar exercises in the past, it has become a routine procedure. The decisions are so automatic that we might have difficulty explaining how we know what to do. There is in fact considerable tacit knowledge that we possess as physics experts that we take for granted but deploy in our reasoning that students are not privy to unless made explicit.

The second factor is largely the answer to the question: Why don't students simply follow the procedures they are taught in class given that they are presented clearly and illustrated with worked out examples? Students have strong and deeply rooted erroneous intuitions about how the physical world works—something that has been known for over four decades through research on "misconceptions." Those intuitions surface in "knee-jerk" fashion when students encounter a situation that they seemingly can explain with their intuitions, and when this happens, what we had taught them in our classes fades to the background. We will discuss this in one of the upcoming chapters in detail. In fact, we will illustrate how students who are able to solve a rather complicated mechanics problem display a major misunderstanding when asked what physicists would deem a simple conceptual question about the physical situation of the problem they just solved. Hence among many students, especially those who find learning physics difficult, there is a constant tension between adopting physicists' ways of thinking and abandoning their experiential (erroneous) intuitive notions. Why? Their intuitions were formed through many experiences and they make sense to them. Young children believe heavy objects fall faster than light object because they do in their worlds from many observations (rocks fall faster than leaves). Newton's Third Law explaining action-reaction is obvious to physicists but try convincing a student that when a 300-pound football linesman tackles them running at full speed, the force that the linesman exerts on them is equal to the force that s/he exerts on the linesman. It is intuitively obvious to the student that they will "feel" the hit more than the linesman will, and they translate that to mean that the larger, heavier object exerts a bigger force on the smaller, lighter object.

1.5. What view undergirds this entire book?

Throughout this book we will promote the view that you should "teach the way you do research." That is, do not work on hunches of what might work well in teaching students difficult concepts and problem solving, but rather, start with research on learning, apply it to classroom instruction, collect data on its effectiveness, and cyclically refine the process. If you must try teaching hunches of what you believe would be effective teaching techniques, evaluate them in terms of evidence of student learning. Teach the way you do research implies that you should let evidence guide you; you can experiment with your teaching but base your approaches on current knowledge about best teaching and learning practices and collect data that allows a determination of whether or not students learned better.

We recognize that instructors are not teaching in isolation—there are situational factors that also impact decisions about what to teach and how to teach it. Perhaps at your institution there is an expectation to do things the way they have always been done, or there is pressure to stay consistent across multiple sections of a course. There might be limitations on the classroom enrollment size and format. Maybe you are afraid that your teaching evaluation scores will go down if you try something new in your classroom. Regardless of your particular situation, another view that undergirds this book is the need for a cultural shift within STEM and especially Physics Departments—we should be supportive of faculty who want to try EBIPs in their classroom, and not hindering progress toward enhanced student learning.

1.6. How are the subsequent chapters of this book organized?

We have taken the view that faculty members are busy people who must manage their professional time between teaching, service and scholarly research. To simplify things we have organized every chapter into three sections, answering the following three questions: (1) What does the research tell us? Here, we will discuss salient research about the chapter's topic, (2) What are the implications of the research for instruction? Here, we interpret the research into a few simple messages about what we should, and should not be doing, to help students learn in the most effective manner possible, and (3) What are some specific examples of applying the research base to teaching physics? Here, we will provide instructional examples in specific contexts that illustrate ways of structuring instruction that are consistent with research on learning.

Chapter 2 starts with a review of conceptual development and the negative impact of misconceptions in learning physics concepts. Chapter 3 focuses on how learning looks for a novice and implications of expert–novice research on physics teaching and learning. Chapter 4 reviews research on the teaching of problem solving. Chapter 5 reviews active learning strategies for the physics classroom. This is a good place to start if you are unfamiliar with EBIPs or are looking for some quick ideas to enhance your instruction. Chapter 6 addresses student perceptions of learning and their study habits—you might be surprised to learn that several of students' study strategies (such as highlighting or rereading) are not supported by research. Chapter 7 examines the topic of assessment, particularly some recent research on the value of testing for learning and retention. Chapter 8 provides some reflections on this book.

The book can be used in (at least) two ways. As for any book, it can be read "all the way through" cover-to-cover if the reader has the time. That is recommended since each chapter builds on prior chapters and examples build on prior examples. A second way to use the book is as a teaching reference guide by selecting a particular topic/chapter to read. A busy faculty member may want some ideas and insights on how to structure testing in a course, or on ways of helping novice students put aside their naive ideas and adopt the concepts and procedures of physics, which are quite unforgiving if misapplied.

No matter how you choose to use this book, we hope you find it both informative and thought provoking. We have strived for brevity while still providing enough details for the ideas presented to make sense.

Reference

Tobias, S. (1990). *They're not Dumb, They're Different: Stalking the Second Tier*. Tucson, AZ: Research Corporation.

Chapter 2 The Formation of Concepts and How to Fix Broken Ones

2.1. What does research on students' concept formation tell us?

When students take a physics class, they come with a range of prior knowledge and experiences that can affect the way they learn physics. To understand how concepts form and evolve, it helps to begin by discussing the current view of learning, called *constructivism* (Trowbridge *et al.*, 2000; Von Glasersfeld, 1989). Constructivism is useful due to its ability to explain a wide range of human behavior, including concept formation and problem solving. However, to appreciate constructivism, it is best to begin with a brief overview of its predecessor, namely the behaviorist view of learning (see Wikipedia entry on behaviorism for a good summary).

2.1.1. A comparison of behaviorist and constructivist views of learning

The behaviorist approach for teaching a complex task is to break up the task into components, teach each one, and later teach by combining the components to achieve the desired behavior. Thus in the behaviorist view, achieving competence is manifested by the individual exhibiting behavior leading to correct completion of a task; positive reinforcement is used to encourage appropriate behavior and negative reinforcement is used to discourage inappropriate behavior. For example, a dog receives a treat for performing a trick (positive reinforcement); or a dog pays more attention when learning a new trick to avoid its master's displeasure (negative reinforcement).

Behaviorism does not care about two important aspects of human learning, the first being the cognitive mechanisms used by the individual to learn a complex task. Knowing how an individual reasons while completing a complex task would seem important in terms of designing effective instructional strategies; that is, performing sub-components and stringing them together does not add up to the understanding of the entire complex process. The second thing that behaviorism does not care about is whether or not the complex task, or processes leading to its completion, makes sense to the individual or whether or not the individual would be able to appropriately apply what was learned to a related or similar task. These would seem like important considerations because if a complex task makes no sense to an individual, then they will impose their own sense making, which may not be accurate from a scientific standpoint; further, if knowledge learned under behaviorism is so closely bound to the task in which it was learned, then that knowledge is not flexible enough to be applied broadly. Behaviorism is useful for designing certain types of training (e.g., assembling a device, testing for and applying chemicals to a swimming pool) but not for educating a student on the nuances of physics concepts.

The constructivist view of learning holds that individuals actively construct the knowledge they possess from observations and experiences that they encounter (National Research Council, 2000; Piaget, 1978; Vygotsky, 1978). On the surface this view seems obvious, perhaps even trite, since at one level, it says that everyone's knowledge is their own, and built brick by brick throughout life. However, there is an important implication in constructivism for instruction, namely that people are not blank slates when learning new knowledge—the knowledge they already possess impacts all future new knowledge that will be learned. This means that when new knowledge conflicts with the knowledge that a student already possesses, the student is likely not to accept the new knowledge and overwrite resident knowledge. Why is this? Constructing knowledge is a time-intensive, effortful process and the student has a strong attachment to the knowledge they have constructed since it "works" for them in real life. For example, many young students (and some college students) believe that heavy objects fall at a faster rate than light objects. This knowledge is accurate in many situations: a piece of paper falls slower than a rock, a leaf falls slower than an acorn, and a foam ball falls slower than a baseball when both thrown up in the air. A student who has grown up making these accurate observations cannot help but construct the concept that heavy objects fall faster than light objects, especially since it is impossible to turn off the effect of air resistance. When they come to a physics class and the instructor states that all objects fall at the same rate, this new knowledge handed down from authority makes no sense to students, and so they often reject it or perhaps construct it as an exception (e.g., objects fall at the same rate only in physics class). When teaching, we often make generalizations without the accompanying caveats, e.g., all objects fall at the same rate (*in the absence of air resistance*). Similarly, most students enter an introductory physics class believing that, in a collision between a large truck and a compact car, the truck exerts a larger force on the car than the car does on the truck. Students base this on the damage to both vehicles after the collision. When told in physics class that Newton's Third Law states that when two bodies interact the forces they exert on each other are equal and opposite, their intellect thinks "Are you kidding me?!" since they equate force with degree of damage. The challenge for instructors is not only teaching correct scientific concepts, but also eradicating (if that is even possible) students' erroneous notions.

2.1.2. Conceptual difficulties in physics

And so we see the difficulties in teaching many physics concepts to students who come to class with their own private understanding of how the physical world works. By the time students reach our physics classes they have been constructing knowledge for many years in order to organize their experiences and observations so that they make sense and also so that they can be used to make predictions. The corpus of private understandings that students bring to physics class is often incomplete, fragmented, and riddled with preconceptions. When preconceptions are in conflict with scientific concepts they are commonly called *misconceptions* (other names are *naive theories*, and *alternate conceptions*). The interested reader may want to delve into detailed studies of a classic acceleration misconception, in which acceleration is treated by students as if it were velocity. For example, students often describe the acceleration of a ball thrown straight up in the air as diminishing as the ball ascends, becoming zero at the top of the trajectory and increasing again as the ball descends (Clement, 1981; Hestenes *et al.*, 1992; Trowbridge & McDermott, 1980, 1981). If asked to discuss the forces on the same ball, students often state that a strong initial force was imparted on the ball but that this force diminishes as the ball climbs, becoming 0 at the top, and then the force of gravity "takes over" and increases so as to speed up the ball as it descends. This is akin to the medieval theory of "impetus" and has been found in several studies (McCloskey et al., 1980; Clement, 1982; Halloun & Hestenes, 1985). More recent discussions of students' conceptual difficulties can be found in (McDermott & Redish, 1999), and in (Docktor & Mestre, 2014).

Given that misconceptions are deeply rooted and difficult to dislodge, the question becomes: What can instructors do to help students overcome misconceptions? There are two prominent conflicting schools of thought on that issue. The first school of thought on overcoming misconceptions holds that they need to be supplanted with correct scientific concepts, and to do so, requires a conflict/resolution approach (Posner et al., 1982; Strike & Posner, 1992). Within this view the instructor would create dissatisfaction with the student's current concept by pointing out, for example, how it is inconsistent for explaining a wide range of phenomena; at the same time, the new concept needs to be intelligible or the student will not understand it. The instructor then shows the plausibility of the scientific concept and its usefulness in making predictions about physical phenomena. This approach is an all-or-nothing replacement of the misconception, which unfortunately seldom occurs. Studies show that students often display correct understanding shortly after a scientific concept is presented in class only to revert to their private understanding weeks later (Clement, 1982; Halloun & Hestenes, 1985).

A more modern approach, termed "knowledge in pieces" (diSessa, 1993; diSessa & Sherin, 1998; Hammer 1996a, 1996b, 2000; Smith et al., 1994) holds that students' knowledge is made up of many "pieces" (or mental "resources") that are compiled in real time to reason about physical situations, making this view more dynamic. A misconception in this view is due to an error in recalling and compiling (inappropriate) knowledge pieces to yield an (incorrect) explanation. Within this view, the instructor would help students use/compile appropriate knowledge pieces in reasoning. That is, learning concepts within this view is manifested by increased accuracy and consistency in coordinating knowledge pieces to yield accurate explanations of scientific phenomena. Note that eradicating misconceptions from memory is not a goal in the knowledge-in-pieces view, especially since cognitive science is not at a stage to determine whether it is even possible to permanently and consciously forget something that we previously learned. Thus, inappropriate knowledge pieces that could be used in reasoning about physics concepts (e.g., heavy objects fall faster than lighter objects) can co-exist with correct knowledge pieces (e.g., all objects fall at the same rate in the absence of air resistance) so long as they are judiciously coordinated to explain phenomena. For example, explaining why a piece of paper falls faster than a rock (in opposition to all objects falling at the same rate) when held and dropped at arm's length is due to air resistance precluding the paper from falling faster, but if the piece of paper is crumbled into a tight ball, the rate of fall would be perceptibly the same for both objects.

The types of misconceptions mentioned above are the result of students' knowledge construction outside of physics classes. There is also another, more insidious type of misconception consisting of students applying a correct concept learned in physics class to a context in which it does not apply, yielding erroneous reasoning; this type of misconception is compiled from knowledge pieces on-the-fly to reason about situations. In fact, the detailed example that we are about to discuss is such a case, and readers will likely be surprised at the bizarre student behavior that can result. The example will also illustrate how the knowledge-in-pieces view can be used to explain student behavior. The example consists of university students making judgments about realistic motion of two balls rolling side-by-side along different tracks in a race. A surprisingly large number of students taking introductory physics interpreted a piece of physics knowledge incorrectly and coordinated it with other knowledge pieces to form a strong misconception about the results of the race between the two balls. In contrast, physics-naive college students who had not taken introductory physics coordinated "common-sense" knowledge beautifully to reason correctly about the race.

2.1.3. Example: A study with balls and tracks

To unpack this odd behavior, we begin by summarizing the task given to students, with additional details found in the published study (Thaden-Koch et al., 2006). The researchers constructed five computer animations of two balls released simultaneously from the top of two tracks, as shown in Fig. 2.1. Figure 2.1 shows a time-lapsed picture of the position of the balls in the five animations at equal time intervals (labeled sequentially with numbers). The four animations depicting unrealistic motion were not constructed from the researchers' whims, but rather a group of students was given a picture of the two tracks with only Ball A drawn in at equal time intervals in the eight positions shown and students were asked to draw the position of Ball B for the eight time intervals on the second track having the "V" valley. The researchers selected the four most popular erroneous renditions and constructed computer animations of the two balls moving in a race. Note that in Fig. 2.1, animation "e" (the last one) depicts realistic motion with Ball B winning the race by a considerable margin. We will also point out that animation "c" is very peculiar

18   The Science of Learning Physics

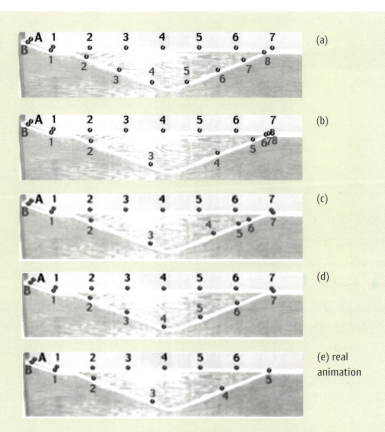

Fig. 2.1. Pictures depicting ball behavior in the animations. Reproduced from *Physical Review: Physics Education Research*, 2006, **2** (#2) 020107 with permission from the American Physical Society.

and unrealistic since it depicts Ball B speeding up on the uphill portion of the "V"; however, this animation is a very popular selection among students who had just finished an introductory physics course—more on why later.

Two groups of students participated in the study, one from an honors calculus-based introductory course (participation took place near the end of the course), and one from an introductory educational psychology course; the educational psychology students had taken no college physics. Students were brought into an office individually and shown two sets of animations. The first set consisted of the five from each group of five that depicted correct, realistic motion of the ball(s). Students had control of playing the animations in whatever order, and however many times they wished (the order of the animations was randomized). After making many comparisons, each student eventually chose one of the five animations as the animation depicting the real, correct motion.

Tables 2.1 and 2.2 show the results, with Table 2.1 showing the selections of the physics students and Table 2.2 the selections of the physics-naive students. At the end of each row is the number of students selecting Ball B animations as realistic and at the bottom of each column is the number of students selecting the animation they believed to be realistic in the two-ball race. Note that for both groups of students, animation "b" and the real animation ("e") were the most popular in judging the motion of Ball B moving alone on the "V" track. This is not surprising: The real animation shows Ball B speeding up on the downhill portion of the "V" and slowing down on the uphill portion. In animation "b" the ball slows down considerably on the uphill portion as if it experienced a lot of rolling friction. Thus we can conclude that generally, students are acting reasonably in attempting to judge realistic motion of one ball moving along a "V" track. Importantly, note that *not a single student chose animation "c" as realistic*, which depicts Ball B speeding up on the uphill portion of the "V".

The surprise comes when looking at the two-ball data (the columns in Tables 2.1 and 2.2). Here, we see that 35% of the physics-naive group chose the realistic animation whereas only 4% (1 student) chose the realistic animation among the

Table 2.1. Animation preferences for 1- and 2-ball tasks, 24 students from Introductory Calculus-based Physics (Honors). Note that entries on the diagonal correspond to students who answer consistently across the 1-ball and 2-ball animations. Reproduced from *Physical Review: Physics Education Research*, 2006, 2 (#2) 020107 with permission from the American Physical Society.

Number choosing 1-ball and 2-ball animations as realistic	2-ball (a)	2-ball (b)	2-ball (c)	2-ball (d)	2-ball (e) (real)	(1-ball) Row Total (percent)
1-ball (a)	-	-	1	1	-	**2** (8%)
1-ball (b)	-	3	7	-	-	**10** (42%)
1-ball (c)	-	-	-	-	-	**0** (0%)
1-ball (d)	-	-	-	-	-	**0** (0%)
1-ball (e) (real)	-	1	7	3	1	**12** (50%)
(2-ball) **Col. Total** (percent)	**0**(0%)	**4**(17%)	**15**(63%)	**4**(17%)	**1**(4%)	**24** (100%)

Table 2.2. Animation preferences for 1- and 2-ball tasks, 26 students from an Educational Psychology class. Note that entries on the diagonal correspond to students who answer consistently across the 1-ball and 2-ball animations. Reproduced from *Physical Review: Physics Education Research*, 2006, 2 (#2) 020107 with permission from the American Physical Society.

Number choosing 1-ball and 2-ball animations as realistic	2-ball (a)	2-ball (b)	2-ball (c)	2-ball (d)	2-ball (e) REAL	(1-ball) Row Total (percent)
1-ball a)	-	3	-	1	2	**7** (23%)
1-ball b)	2	3	-	-	1	**9** (35%)
1-ball c)	-	-	-	-	-	**0** (0%)
1-ball d)	-	-	-	1	-	**1** (4%)
1-ball e) (real)	2	2	-	-	6	**10** (38%)
(2-ball) **Col. Total** (percent)	**4**(15%)	**11**(42%)	**0**(0%)	**2**(8%)	**9**(35%)	**26** (100%)

physics students. Even more bizarre, *we see now that 63% of the physics students chose animation "c" as realistic* (the one showing Ball B speeding up while going uphill), whereas not a single physics-naive student chose animation "c" as realistic. The researchers report that when viewing the single-ball animations for Ball B, a lot of students from both groups laughed when viewing animation "c" and dismissed it outright as unrealistic—after all, who would think that a ball would speed up going uphill without a cause. Yet, no physics student laughed when viewing the two ball "c" animation, and the majority of them selected it as realistic. What reasoning could have led to this bizarre behavior?

During the experiment, students were asked to "think aloud" while making their decisions about realistic motion—that is, they were asked to verbalize the reasoning that led to their choice of realistic motion, and the entire session was audio-recorded for later analysis. Generally, the reasoning of both groups showed correct "knowledge pieces" brought to bear on the situation. For example, students from both groups expected Ball B to speed up on the downhill and to slow down on the uphill. The bizarre behavior of 63% of the physics students selecting animation "c" in the two-ball race as realistic stemmed from the inappropriate application of a physics concept learned in class, namely conservation of mechanical energy. Those students reasoned that both balls were released from the same height, and returned to the same height at the end of the race, and that by conservation of energy they had to have the same speed at the end and thus they had to tie at the end. Note that these "knowledge pieces" as applied by the physics students are all correct except for the conclusion that equal speeds at the end implies equal positions at the end. Interestingly, the physics students invoking this argument were looking for a tie result at the end of the race, and only two animations had tie results (c and d); but animation "d" did not meet the criteria of Ball B speeding up on the downhill and slowing down on the uphill. The researchers also reported that for many physics students invoking this argument, looking for a tie outcome precluded them from noticing Ball B speeding up in the uphill portion in the two-ball race.

There are several take-away messages from this study. First, when learning a physics concept for the first time, students can misinterpret or overextend the implications of the concept, leading to erroneous reasoning. Second, having a strong expectation from an incorrect application of a concept can lead to not noticing important features of a situation (in this case, a ball speeding up while going uphill). Third, students coordinate pieces of knowledge "on-the-fly" to reason about situations, as the knowledge in pieces view asserts. Finally, and on the positive side, the physics students in this study did try to apply physics knowledge that they learned in class, but unfortunately, lacking the expert's perspective they were prone to overextend or misapply the conservation of mechanical energy concept.

2.2. What are the implications of research on students' concept formation for instruction?

We offer the following implications of the research reviewed above for instruction:

- Students come to our classes with preconceptions that often interfere with the physics concepts that we try to teach them. Students construct their own private understandings of the physical world around them through observations and experiences. The preconceptions formed by this process are often misconceptions that

run counter to correct physics concepts. Because it takes time and mental energy to construct concepts, students' misconceptions are deeply rooted and resistant to change. It is important for instructors to be on the lookout for students' misconceptions since they interfere with the learning of physics concepts. More on available inventories to identify misconceptions provided in the Teaching Interventions section below.
- **"Teaching by telling" will likely not be sufficient to help students overcome misconceptions.** Although the lecture method of instruction is effective for some students, learning via this method is rather passive and allows little opportunity for students to construct knowledge. Methods that offer more engagement are better suited for knowledge construction. If a student possesses a misconception it becomes even more important to engage the student in reconstructing appropriate conceptual understanding. When listening to an instructor discuss a concept that conflicts with previously constructed knowledge, a student is not likely to give up their own private understanding and replace it with the instructor's version.
- **Nuanced understanding about the meaning and appropriate application of a concept takes time and multiple contextual experiences.** The example provided above with the two rolling balls in a race along two tracks of different shapes shows that students often overextend or misinterpret the applicability of a concept. When presenting a new concept, instructors should discuss both, the contexts in which the concept applies, as well as the more salient contexts in which it does not apply to allow students to build a rich contextual knowledge base of the concept's applicability.

- **Some misconceptions are easier to overcome than others.** Misconceptions that have been held for a long period of time and which work in predicting physical outcomes in the world we live in (e.g., heavy objects fall faster than light objects, as in a rock falls faster than a leaf) are harder to reconstruct than others that are formed on-the-fly by compiling correct with incorrect knowledge pieces. The balls-on-tracks example above is an example of the latter case where students compile in real time some correct knowledge pieces (e.g., the balls will have the same speed in the final shelf due to conservation of mechanical energy) with incorrect knowledge pieces (e.g., having the same speed at the end implies the balls will arrive at the same time). It is much easier for students to "fix" incorrect knowledge pieces than to abandon long-held misconceptions that have observable verification in our messy "real world" (e.g., heavy objects fall faster than light objects).
- **Expect some students to exhibit appropriate understanding of a physics concept immediately after teaching it but to revert to an associated misconception they possess related to the concept weeks later.** It is common to have students exhibit understanding of physics conceptual questions when tested shortly following instruction only to have misconceptions on the concept return when tested weeks later. From a constructivist viewpoint, recall that students construct their own private understanding of the concept from observations and the constructed concept makes sense to the student in terms of making predictions about the physical world. It is difficult for students to give up their constructed knowledge after a short exposure to a physicist's presentation of the concept. From a knowledge-in-pieces perspective, the student has numerous knowledge

pieces in memory, some correct (e.g., concepts taught in physics class) and some incorrect (misconceptions from observing the physical world), and which piece of knowledge gets activated in memory is highly context dependent.
- **Misconceptions are difficult to uproot but instructors can take steps to help students construct appropriate understanding of physics concepts.** It is unlikely that one can ever consciously *erase* one's own memory of a misconception once formed. However, with the help of instructors, one can always learn to *cope* with it. By pointing out the different contexts in which a concept holds and the contexts in which it does not, by pointing out how a students' misconception might be valid under certain conditions but not universally, and by helping students compile appropriate knowledge pieces to reason about situations, instructors can help students become aware of common pitfalls and develop a conceptual knowledge base suitable for doing physics.

2.3. Examples of teaching interventions based on learning research

The research reviewed in this chapter, as well as our teaching experiences, indicate that students are not blank slates when it comes to having their own private "theories" about how the physical world works. It is therefore important to probe for students' conceptual understanding during the course of instruction so that we can identify misconceptions and help students restructure their knowledge to reason effectively about the physical world.

- Implement active learning (more details on active learning in Chapter 5). Active learning takes many forms, but essentially, it consists of getting students actively engaged in constructing knowledge (e.g., using conceptual "clicker" questions in large classes where students discuss and then answer them in small collaborative groups). Although active learning is not guaranteed to perfect students' conceptual understanding, it does offer many benefits. For example, it allows instructors to probe for misconceptions. Further, it also allows students and instructors to openly discuss how misconceptions result in an inconsistent description of the physical world and sets the stage for students reconstructing knowledge. Although not causal, there is strong correlational evidence that courses taught using active learning strategies result in fewer misconceptions following instruction compared to more traditional methods of instruction (Hake, 1998; Freeman *et al.*, 2014). Such evidence comes from administering a conceptual inventory (designed to probe for misconceptions using multiple-choice questions) prior to, and following instruction and comparing the pre-to-post gains in performance. There are about a dozen commonly used conceptual inventories in introductory physics, among the most popular being the Force Concept Inventory (Hestenes *et al.*, 1992) and the Force and Motion Conceptual Evaluation (Thornton & Sokoloff, 1998). A quick reference guide of other conceptual inventories in physics is found on page 24 in (Docktor & Mestre, 2014).

We now provide two examples of question sequences that have been used in large lectures by one of us (JPM) using clicker technologies both to identify specific misconceptions and to help students build appropriate conceptual knowledge. The first example uses a classroom demonstration where a spring scale has two light strings attached at either end, one end attached to a stationary hook and the other going over a pulley and attached to a known weight. Figure 2.3 shows the situation. We present the demo to students without first hanging the weight, and demonstrate that the harder we pull on the string at the right, the higher the reading on the scale. Then we cover the scale with a cloth, hang the known weight, and ask the following multiple choice question for students to discuss in small groups (note that the cloth is not shown in Fig. 2.3).

When answers are collected with the clickers, not surprisingly, all students answer correctly—4 lbs. Next we change the context slightly by covering the scale with the cloth again, removing the left end from the hook, attaching another 4 lbs weight to that end, and putting the string over a second pulley at the left end so that both weights hang without moving with the veiled scale in the middle. Figure 2.4 shows the new set up and the question asked (note that the cloth over the scale is not shown in Fig. 2.4).

If you guessed that the majority now answer 8 lbs, you would be correct. (If you are not a physicist reading this and are surprised, the answer does not change from before.) Most students now think that hanging an equal weight from both sides doubles the force reading on the scale and the tension in the strings. They reason that gravity is pulling with 4 lbs on each side, which adds up to 8 lbs—visually this seems reasonable to them without analyzing the situation with Newton's Second Law. Note that they reasoned perfectly fine in the first case, thinking that gravity pulls with 4 lbs and thus the scale must read that amount since the string attached to the weight is holding 4 lbs and thus pulls the scale with that force since the weight remains in equilibrium. Yet, in the second case, the weight hanging on the right is still in equilibrium, so as far as the scale is concerned, nothing

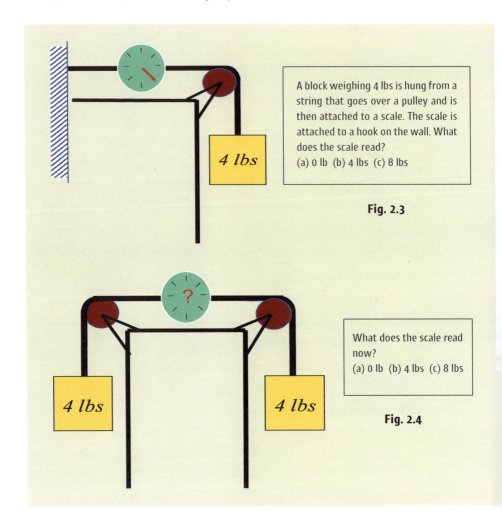

Fig. 2.3

Fig. 2.4

has changed. This offers an opportunity for the instructor to refine students' understanding by helping them analyze the two hanging weights using Newton's Second Law, showing that previously the hook provided the 4 lbs force needed to keep the scale and weight in equilibrium, and in the second case the 4 lbs weight on the left serves that same purpose. One can also pose the argument to students that, if this weren't so, there would be a major contradiction with Newton's Second Law: If the scale read 8 lbs, then the two strings to either side of the scale would have 8 lbs of tension, so that now, for both hanging weights, there would be an unbalanced force of 4 lbs acting vertically up on the masses, and thus they both would magically have to accelerate upwards!

Another two-question set also serves to highlight a common misconception and ways of addressing it. The first question presents a physical situation consisting of two blocks of different masses in contact with each other on a slippery horizontal table having different forces applied from each side, and asked for the acceleration of the blocks, as shown in Fig. 2.5.

Students are invited to discuss the question with their neighbors and to answer when done. Not surprisingly, following instruction on Newton's Second Law, very few students get this question wrong after answers are collected with clickers. When asked to volunteer their reasoning, students argue correctly that the two blocks can be considered a "body" for analysis with Newton's Second Law, and then add the two forces vectorially to arrive at a net force of 12 N toward the right, which when divided by the total mass of 4 kg yields the 3 m/s^2 acceleration.

The surprise and conflict comes when asked the follow-up question shown in Fig. 2.6. Now misconceptions magically surface, as students abandon Newton's Second Law and resort to knee-jerk seemingly-reasonable answers that are flat-out wrong. Students choosing choice [(a) and (b)] argue that the force on the left (right) applied to the 3 kg (1 kg) block just "goes right through" the block. Those answering (c) argue that the force in the middle between the blocks is the difference of the forces acting at the two ends. Those answering 16 N argue that the force in the middle is the sum of the two forces since the middle is being squashed by the two end forces. What is crucially

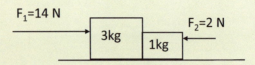

In the situation shown, two horizontal external forces are applied to the two blocks as shown. There is no friction. What is the acceleration of the blocks?
(a) 4 m/s² (b) 8 m/s² (c) 3 m/s² (d) 3.67 m/s²

Fig. 2.5

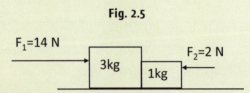

In the situation shown, two horizontal external forces are applied to the two blocks as shown. There is no friction. What is the force that the 1 kg block exerts on the 3 kg block, $F_{on\ 3\ by\ 1}$? Recall that a = 3 m/s².
(a) 14 N (b) 2 N (c) 12 N (d) 16 N (e) 5 N

Fig. 2.6

important to note is that in the first question, students applied Newton's Second Law flawlessly to arrive at a correct answer. And so the question becomes: Why did they so quickly abandon Newton's Second Law to analyze the second situation? Had they identified the 3 kg block as the body of interest, drawn a free-body diagram of the forces on it, and analyzed it the same way they analyzed the two blocks in the first question, it would have inevitably led them to the correct answer of 5 N given that they know the acceleration of each block from the first question.

Note that in both of these examples, two slightly different contexts were used, with the second context tempting students to abandon the physics presented in class in favor of their own knee-jerk reasoning. The second question in each set created conflict in students' minds, which with guidance from the instructor could be resolved with appropriate physics reasoning. One of us who has used these examples in class likes to add humor to these situations during class by asking students "Did I ever teach you 'Newton's Difference of Two Forces Law' that states that when confronted with two forces, just add them or subtract them?" or "Did I ever teach you 'Newton's the-force-goes-right-through-a-body Law'?" Students laugh, but questions like these prove the point that physics in unforgiving unless one plays by the rules. Examples like these also serve to caution students not to fall prey to their knee-jerk intuitions and to instead rely on analyses using physics concepts taught in class.

- **Implement formative assessment classroom techniques to elicit students' ideas.** Formative assessment techniques (i.e., assessment in the service of learning rather than for assigning grades) include a host of different low-stakes strategies for making students' thinking more visible to the instructor (Keeley, 2008). You're probably familiar with *think-pair-share* where a student first thinks about a question on their own, talks to a partner, and then shares ideas with the class. This general strategy could be implemented with the conceptual clicker questions addressed in the previous bullet. Other strategies include using mini whiteboards during class, giving students time during class to pause and write/summarize the lesson so far or identify the muddiest point, concept mapping, or focused listing where a student brainstorms everything they already know about a particular topic at the beginning of a new unit. If you teach a physics course for future teachers, the book series *Understanding Student Ideas in Science* by Page Keeley contains hundreds of formative assessment probes on K-12 topics that can also be used with college students. For example, when provided with a list of objects and asked which ones will stick to a magnet, most pre-service teachers will say that *all* metals stick to a magnet. Even after conducting several investigations where they observe that magnets do not stick to a piece of aluminum foil or a copper pipe, students will often revert to their original ideas. When asked whether they will be able to see an apple in a completely dark room, many students will say that their eyes will eventually adjust to see the outline of the apple or an apple without color, even when there is no light for their eyes to detect. These examples illustrate that many of the misconceptions that start in young children permeate into adulthood.

- **Implement other instructional strategies specifically designed to identify and address students' misconceptions.** There are other specific strategies to help students overcome common stubborn misconceptions. We discuss briefly two of them here but the reader may wish to read more in the Docktor and Mestre synthesis of physics education research (2014). The Washington University's Physics Education Group's *Tutorials in Introductory Physics* (McDermott & Shaffer, 2002) offers a supplementary curriculum for use in small group discussion sections, although they can be adapted for use in lecture settings. The curriculum consists of "modules" treating specific topics (e.g., velocity & acceleration, Newton's Laws, geometric optics, gas laws) and the modules consist of pretests, worksheets and homework assignments designed to identify misconceptions and to help students overcome them. A second approach for use in large lecture settings are the Interactive Lecture Demonstrations (ILD) (Sokoloff & Thornton, 2004). This curriculum combines lecture demonstrations with conceptual development through a specific sequence of instructional activities. The activities start by introducing a lecture demonstration, then asking students to make a prediction on the outcomes after discussing with peers, then they see the actual demonstration (usually showing erroneous reasoning by a large portion of students), and then attempt to reach resolution on the concepts underlying the lecture demonstration. Each stage in this approach is guided by questions in hand-out worksheets. Studies on the effectiveness of ILDs show significant improvements in the understanding of basic physics concepts as measured by the FMCE. Another approach is the use of bridging analogies and anchoring intuitions to lead students to appropriate conceptions (Clement, 1998). For example, to address the common misconception that passive objects like tables cannot exert a force, a lesson can start with an *anchoring example* that triggers the correct conception: when a hand pushes down on a spring, the spring pushes back on the hand. Then a series of *bridging analogies* are used and discussed: a book resting on a piece of foam, a book resting on a long flexible board, and finally a book resting on a rigid table. Demonstrations can be used with lasers and mirrors to illustrate that even a "rigid" table undergoes small deformations when an object is placed on top of it, and eventually the lesson can include a microscopic model of atoms in a solid having spring-like bonds between them. These approaches, as well as others, have commonalities, such as creating conflict between students' current understanding and the targeted physics concept, and then guiding students through the resolution of the conflict. They also offer opportunities for discussing concepts in multiple contexts.

References

Clement, J.J. (1981). Solving problems with formulas: Some limitations. *Engineering Education*, **72**, 158–162.

Clement, J.J. (1982). Students' preconceptions in introductory mechanics. *American Journal of Physics*, **50**, 66–71.

Clement, J.J. (1998). Expert novice similarities and instruction using analogies. *International Journal of Science Education*, **20**(10), 1271–1286.

diSessa, A.A. (1993). Toward an epistemology of physics. *Cognition and Instruction*, **10**, 105–225.

diSessa, A.A. & Sherin, B.L., (1998). What changes in conceptual change? *International Journal of Science Education*, **20**(10), 1155–1191.

Docktor, J.L. & Mestre, J.P. (2014). Synthesis of discipline-based education research in physics. *Physical Review Special Topics – Physics Education Research*, **10**(2), 020119 (58 pages). doi: 10.1103/PhysRevSTPER.10.020119

Freeman, S., Eddy, S.L., McDonough, M., Smith, M.K., Okoroafor, N., Jordt, H. & Wenderoth, M.P. (2014). Active learning increases student performance in science, engineering, and mathematics. *Proceedings of the National Academy of Sciences*, **111**(23), 8410–8415. doi: 10.1073/pnas.1319030111

Hake, R.R. (1998). Interactive-engagement versus traditional methods: A six-thousand student survey of mechanics test data for introductory physics courses. *American Journal of Physics*, **66**, 64–74.

Halloun, I.A. & Hestenes, D. (1985). The initial knowledge state of college physics students. *American Journal of Physics*, **53**, 1043–1055.

Hammer, D. (1996a). Misconceptions or p-prims: How might alternative perspectives on cognitive structure influence instructional perceptions and intentions. *Journal of the Learning Sciences*, **5**, 97–127.

Hammer, D. (1996b). More than misconceptions: Multiple perspectives on student knowledge and reasoning, and an appropriate role for education research. *American Journal of Physics*, **64**(10), 1316–1325.

Hammer, D. (2000). Student resources for learning introductory physics. *American Journal of Physics*, **68**, S52–S59.

Hestenes, D., Wells, M. & Swackhamer, G. (1992). Force concept inventory. *The Physics Teacher*, **30**, (March), 159–166.

Keeley, P.D. (2008). *Science Formative Assessment: 75 Practical Strategies for Linking Assessment, Instruction, and Learning*. NSTA Press.

McCloskey, M., Caramazza, A. & Green, B. (1980). Curvilinear motion in the absence of external forces: Naive beliefs about the motion of objects. *Science*, **210**, 1139–1141.

McDermott, L.C. & Shaffer, P.S. (2002). *Tutorials in Introductory Physics*. Prentice-Hall, Upper Saddle River, NJ.

McDermott, L.C. & Redish, E.F.(1999). Resource letter: PER-1: Physics education research. *American Journal of Physics*, **67**, 755–767.

National Research Council (2000). *How People Learn: Brain, Mind, Experience, and School: Expanded Edition*. Washington, DC: The National Academies Press. https://doi.org/10.17226/9853

Piaget, J. (1978). *Success and Understanding*. Cambridge, MA: Harvard University Press.

Posner, G., Strike, K., Hewson, P. & Gerzog, W. (1982). Accommodation of a scientific conception: Toward a theory of conceptual change. *Science Education*, **66**, 211–227.

Smith, J., diSessa, A. & Roschelle, J. (1994) Misconceptions reconceived: A constructivist analysis of knowledge in transition. *Journal of the Learning Sciences*, **3**, 115–163.

Sokoloff, D.R. & Thornton, R.K. (2004). *Interactive Lecture Demonstrations, Active Learning in Introductory Physics*. John Wiley & Sons, Hoboken, NJ.

Strike, K.A. & Posner, G.J. (1992). A revisionist theory of conceptual change. In *Philosophy of Science, Cognitive Psychology, and Educational Theory and Practice*. In R.A. Duschl and R.J. Hamilton (Eds.) pp. 147–176, State University of New York Press, New York.

Thaden-Koch, T., Dufresne, R. & Mestre, J. (2006). Coordination of knowledge in judging animated motion. *Physical Review Special*

Topics: Physics Education Research, 2(2), 020107 (11 pages). doi: 10.1103/PhysRevSTPER.2.020107

(http://prst-per.aps.org/pdf/PRSTPER/v2/i2/e020107)

Thornton, R.K. & Sokoloff, D.R. (1998). Assessing student learning of Newton's laws: The force and motion conceptual evaluation and the evaluation of active learning laboratory and lecture curricula, *American Journal of Physics*, **66**, 338–352.

Trowbridge, L.W., Bybee, R.W. & Powell, J.C. (2000). *Teaching Secondary School Science: Strategies for Developing Scientific Literacy*, 7th ed. Prentice-Hall, Upper Saddle River, NJ.

Trowbridge, D.E. & McDermott, L.C. (1980). Investigation of student understanding of the concept of velocity in one dimension. *American Journal of Physics*, **48**, 1020–1028.

Trowbridge, D.E. & McDermott, L.C. (1981). Investigation of student understanding of the concept of acceleration in one dimension. *American Journal of Physics*, **49**, 242–253.

Von Glasersfeld, E. (1989). Cognition, construction of knowledge, and teaching. *Synthese*, **80**, 121–140.

Vygotsky, L.S. (1978). *Mind in Society: The Development of Higher Psychological Processes*. Cambridge, MA: The Harvard University Press. (Originally published 1930, New York: Oxford University Press.)

Chapter

3 How Learning Looks for a Novice:
Implications of Expert–Novice Research for Physics Teaching and Learning

3.1. What does expert–novice research tell us?

To understand how students taking introductory physics behave in terms of solving problems, it helps to review findings from the study of expertise, not because our job as instructors is necessarily to turn those students into experts, but because how experts and novices organize knowledge in memory and deploy it to solve problems is quite different, and provides a window into novices' minds. The first thing that becomes evident as one begins to learn a new area is that one lacks perspective on what is important. We have all had experiences where we have felt like a novice—perhaps learning to play a musical instrument, or learning a new sport or complicated board game. For example, in learning to play golf for the first time, should one swing the club like a baseball bat only downwards? Should one swing the different clubs the same way? Should one keep the arms flexible during a swing or keep one arm stiff? Should one twist one's hips when swinging or keep them facing the ball during the entire swing? Does one get more power by swinging harder? Answers to these questions can be surprising to a novice, and in fact, preconceived answers to these questions can get in the way, making progress in learning the game. For example, the answer to the last question is no—power (length that the ball travels for a given club) is about technique, not strength of swing. One of us who's a "journeyman" in golf can attest to witnessing scrawny guys and gals hitting very long shots indeed due to their excellent form, whereas muscly guys who swing hard (with poor technique) usually hit embarrassingly short shots. As one plays more and more, one starts to gain perspective on what is important, and then comes refinement. The same is true for learning physics—we begin to notice the subtleties of "playing the physics game," the more we learn physics.

3.1.1. Broad observations about novices and experts in physics

Lacking any perspective on what is important in physics, a beginner treats every new concept or equation encountered in an introductory course as equally important (or unimportant). All concepts, equations and facts are thrown into memory with little by way of organization other than perhaps the order in which they are covered or the context in which they are presented in the course. Solving problems is usually a pattern-matching exercise for the novice, hunting for equations whose variables match those given in the problem, and then blindly plugging in values to generate an answer. We have all witnessed this behavior and wonder why our students do not organize knowledge and use it to solve problems "our way," or the way we try to teach them, namely to start with an analysis of the problem and decide what "big idea" applies, and then to move towards specifics such as the equation(s) and procedure(s) that go with the application of the big idea. In fact, physicists will likely agree that in an introductory mechanics course there are only four big ideas covered (Newton's Second Law, work-energy theorem and conservation of mechanical energy, impulse-momentum theorem and conservation of momentum, and angular impulse-angular momentum theorem and conservation of angular momentum) and a few secondary ideas (e.g., kinematics, the other two Newton Laws). Yet introductory physics students are always complaining to us that there is so much to remember, meaning the hundred-some-odd equations they encounter in a typical course, which is largely a consequence of poorly organized physics knowledge in memory. When experts activate a physics concept or principle, the particular concept/principle in memory is "attached" to a procedure(s)/equation(s) for applying it; this makes remembering the plethora of equations needed in physics problem solving easy for the expert since their entire memory store is organized efficiently (National Research Council, 2000). It is important to be patient with our novice students, since it is not that they are trying to be obstinate—they are just behaving in the way that all novices behave. After all, those who study expertise state that it takes about 10,000 hours to become an expert at something (Ericsson *et al.*, 1993), and by the end of one semester of introductory physics, our best students are only about 140 hours into it (assuming that they are diligent and spend ~10 hours/week during the entire 14-week semester—granted an optimistic estimate).

Although the research literature typically classifies participants as either "novices" or "experts," it is important to note that the development of expertise occurs across a continuum. Dreyfus and Dreyfus (1986) describe five stages of skill acquisition. A *novice* is someone who is still learning the facts and rules of a skill; their decision-making process is very deliberate and tasks require full concentration. With more experience, a novice progresses to the stage of *advanced beginner*, or someone who bases their decisions on similar situations they have encountered. As the beginner starts to organize situation features into a hierarchy of important elements and base their decisions on the presence or absence of particular features, they are labeled as *competent*. Someone who is *proficient* at a skill has an intuitive ability to recognize important features of a task and organize information, but still consciously analyzes the available options. Finally, an *expert* on tasks that are routine for them will make automatic, intuitive decisions. Another proficiency scale cited in (Chi, 2006) is novice, initiate, apprentice, journeyman, expert, and master.

3.1.2. Some important expert–novice differences

There are a number of salient expert–novice differences in physics. One of the earliest studies of expertise in physics (Chi *et al.*, 1981) was a problem categorization study where physics novices (college students who had completed a mechanics course) and experts (physics graduate students) were given 24 mechanics problems written on individual 3×5 cards and asked to sort the problems into piles according to similarity of solution (without solving them first). The piles made by novices and experts had distinctly different features: Novices' piles shared surface similarities based on objects/configurations (e.g., blocks on inclined plane problems were in one pile), and/or physics terms (e.g., friction problems were in a pile); experts' piles shared the major physics principle that would be used to solve the problems (e.g., Newton's Second Law, conservation of energy). The categorization criteria used by experts and novices were not solely along the surface features or principles but fell largely along those dimensions. That same study also asked novices and experts to discuss the "basic approach" that would be used to solve a set of problems. The surface attributes and statements in the problems cued tacit knowledge in experts that allowed them to access appropriate principles and procedures that could be applied to solve the problems; in contrast, novices used surface attributes to look for equations that seemed appropriate (e.g., matching quantities given in the problems to quantities in equations). This equation-based approach, often called "means–ends analysis," attempts to reduce the "distance" between the givens in the problem and the goal state. It is described by Larkin *et al.* (1980) as follows: "Means–ends analysis begins with the desired quantity and looks for equations including that quantity. Then it works backward, marking as desired any unbound quantity needed to solve such an equation." (See also articles by Van Heuvelen and Maloney (1999) and by Sweller (2011).) You may have also heard this approach referred to as "plug-and-chug" problem solving (Walsh *et al.*, 2007) or a search-based strategy (Gick, 1986). Students might also use a "memory-based" approach by mimicking the solution to a similar problem they have seen. A major shortcoming of this method of solving problems commonly employed by novices in physics is that it requires substantial mental resources on the part of the solver (termed "memory load"), hence leaving few mental resources for conceptual learning.

3.1.3. Differences in what novices and experts notice when "doing" physics

These findings indicate that what is noticed in physics problems and situations is highly dependent on expertise. In particular, experts notice important attributes in a physics situation and use tacit knowledge to interpret the situation; lacking extensive knowledge, important features of situations go unnoticed by novices. For example, a study using eye-tracking (technology that tracks eye movements while an individual performs a task) revealed marked differences between those who answered physics questions correctly and those who didn't (Madsen et al., 2012). All problems used had a diagram, and a conceptual question was asked while participants' eyes were tracked as they looked at the diagrams and answered the question. Those who answered the questions correctly spent a larger proportion of time looking at thematically-relevant portions of the diagrams, whereas those who answered incorrectly spent considerably more time looking at diagram features that contained salient surface-feature attributes but that were not thematically relevant for answering the question. For example, one problem had roller coaster cars traveling along different frictionless paths and ending at the same height from which they started; people who correctly answered a question about the speed at the end focused their attention on just the initial and final heights of the cars (which were "thematically relevant" for an energy approach) whereas people who answered incorrectly focused more visual attention on the paths that the cars traveled.

Another recent study using a phenomenon called "change blindness" from the cognitive psychology subfield of visual cognition provides additional strong evidence for how novices and experts direct their attention. Change blindness explores what people notice during a change in a situation—for example, a participant might be shown a picture on a screen, then distracted from looking at it for a moment, during which something is purposely changed in the picture, and then one ascertains if the participant noticed the change. Another paradigm uses person-change events; for example, an unsuspecting participant walks up to a counter and interacts briefly with a person behind the counter, then the person behind the counter finds an excuse to duck below the counter (e.g., supposedly looking for a paper form the participant needs), and a *different* person pops up and continues the interaction. In about half the instances, the unsuspecting participant does not notice that the person behind the counter changed (if you want to be amused, search for "change blindness person change events" on YouTube and witness such experiments). The physics study (Feil & Mestre, 2010) brought unsuspecting experts (physics graduate students) and novices (students who had finished a mechanics course) to an office where an experimenter showed a participant a computer screen with a physics situation and asked the participant to formulate an explanation for the behavior of an object in the situation. After the participant was ready to offer their explanation, the participant was purposely distracted for a moment and the experimenter clicked on a hidden wireless mouse that changed the situation on the screen slightly. Two different situations were used, one where the change made did not alter the underlying physics needed to explain the behavior of the situation, and one where the change did impact the underlying physics. Figure 3.1 contains the original and changed diagrams for the two situations used.

Somewhat surprisingly, in Situation 1, **none** of the 31 experts or 48 novices who participated in the study noticed the ramp-shape change when they looked back at the screen and started to explain how they would go about finding the maximum compression of the spring. Note that the ramp-shape change did not change the underlying physics needed for the explanation; the explanation that experts had formulated, based on conservation of energy, could be used to explain how the maximum

44 The Science of Learning Physics

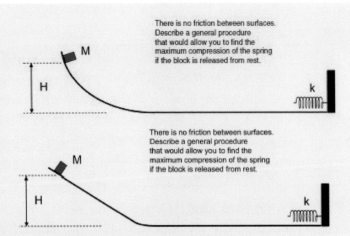

Situation 1: Top diagram was the original and bottom diagram was the changed diagram.

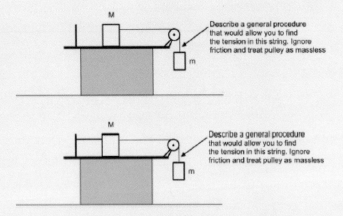

Situation 2: Top diagram was the original and bottom diagram was the changed diagram.

Fig. 3.1. Diagrams used in change blindness study.

compression of the spring could be found in both ramp situations, and hence when they internalized the situation in terms of the underlying physics, the physics principle needed for explaining the situation remained the same for both cases, which did not lead to any *conceptual* inconsistency. This was not the case for Situation 2, where adding a string that tied the block on the table to the wall changed the behavior of the system drastically. In this situation, 77% of the experts noticed the change, with the vast majority of them showing surprise and stating that they had "missed" the string attaching mass M to the wall when they had initially viewed the diagram and formulated an explanation (perhaps, it is also surprising that *only* 77% of the experts noticed). In contrast, only 27% of the novices noticed the added string. Thus experts noticed that the change made to the situation changed the physics at about three times the rate as novices. In fact, the behavior and explanations offered by novices who noticed the string addition were indistinguishable from the experts that noticed it. In summary, novices and experts generally notice and attend to different things in physics situations.

3.1.4. Problem solving differences between novices and experts in physics

Another difference between experts and novices is how they approach problem solving. A novice behavior that all physics instructors have witnessed is that when solving problems, novices hunt for equations that contain the variables/quantities given in the problem. In contrast, experts begin by conducting basic-level descriptions and qualitative analyses of the problem based on the major concepts and principles needed for constructing a solution (Reif & Heller, 1982). Once identified, the expert knows what procedure and equation(s) are typically used to apply the concept. These observations were also identified in (Chi *et al.*, 1981) a study cited earlier. In fact, one of us (JM) who often taught discussion sections at the University of Illinois, during which students would solve difficult, "capstone" problems in collaborative groups, would typically ask the foursome in a group what "big idea" they had applied to solve a problem they had just finished. Students would have the look of a "deer in the headlights" for a few seconds, and then start reporting what equation(s) they had used in solving the problem. It was only near the middle to end of the course that students started catching on to what was meant by the big idea being applied to solve problems.

3.1.5. Can instruction be designed to promote expert-like behavior in physics?

3.1.5.1. Short-term interventions

Expert–novice research in physics also indicates that some novices (those who learn physics easily) can behave like experts, findings that are evident in the change blindness study described above. This leads to the question: Can expert-like behavior in physics be taught to novices so that they begin to exhibit such behavior. Some studies suggest a qualified "yes."

An early study (Dufresne et al., 1992) attempted to answer the question of whether or not constraining novices, after they had finished an introductory course and received a respectable grade (B or better), to perform expert-like analyses of problems prior to solving them resulted in manifestations of expert-like behavior. As educational experiments go, this one was complicated since it required that the participants practice an expert-like problem solving approach long enough for it to "take hold." The experiment took place over 9 one-hour sessions spread over about 3 weeks, and participants were students who had finished an introductory mechanics course with a grade of B or better. The expert-like approach used to train students draws from the research reviewed earlier in this chapter, namely that experts begin by identifying major principles/concepts needed to solve problems, and then move toward the procedure(s) and equation(s) needed for solution. Thus a rudimentary menu-driven, computer-based "hierarchical analysis tool" or HAT was constructed that would allow novices to analyze problems by first identifying one of the four major principles covered in the introductory mechanics course needed for solving the problem (in the first menu), and then to continue refining the analysis through subsequent menus until at the end of the analysis one or more equations were provided that could be used to solve the problem.

A small block of mass M slides along a track having both curved and horizontal sections as shown. If the block is released from rest at height H, what is its speed when it is on the horizontal section of the track? The track is frictionless.

Which principle applies to this part of the problem solution?
    1. Newton's Second Law or Kinematics
    2. Angular Momentum
    3. Linear Momentum
    4. Work and Energy
Please enter your selection: [4]
(B)ackup (M)ain menu (G)lossary (L)ist selections (Q)uit

Describe the system in terms of its mechanical energy.
    1. Conservative system (conservation of energy)
    2. Non-conservative system
Please enter your selection: [1]
(B)ackup (M)ain menu (G)lossary (L)ist selections (Q)uit

(Continued)

Describe the changes in mechanical energy. Consider only the energy of one body at a time at some initial and final state.
   1. Change in kinetic energy
   2. Change in potential energy
   3. Change in potential and kinetic energy
Please enter your selection: [3]
(B)ackup   (M)ain menu   (G)lossary   (L)ist selections   (Q)uit

Describe the changes in kinetic energy.
   1. Change in translational kinetic energy
   2. Change in rotational kinetic energy
   3. Change in translational and rotational kinetic energies
Please enter your selection: [1]
(B)ackup   (M)ain menu   (G)lossary   (L)ist selections   (Q)uit

Describe the boundary conditions.
   1. No initial translational kinetic energy
   2. No final translational kinetic energy
   3. Initial and final translational kinetic energies
Please enter your selection: [1]
(B)ackup   (M)ain menu   (G)lossary   (L)ist selections   (Q)uit

Describe the changes in potential energy.
   1. Changes in gravitational potential energy
   2. Changes in spring potential energy
   3. Changes in gravitational and spring potential energy
Please enter your selection: [1]
(B)ackup   (M)ain menu   (G)lossary   (L)ist selections   (Q)uit

Describe the boundary conditions.
   1. No initial gravitational potential energy
   2. No final gravitational potential energy
   3. Initial and final gravitational potential energy
Please enter your selection: [2]
(B)ackup   (M)ain menu   (G)lossary   (L)ist selections   (Q)uit

(Continued)

> **Is there another body in the system which has not been examined?**
>   1. Yes
>   2. No
>
> Please enter your selection: [2]
> (B)ackup (M)ain menu (G)lossary (L)ist selections (Q)uit
>
> **The Work–Kinetic Energy Theorem states that the work done on the system by all non-conservative forces is equal to the change in the mechanical energy of the system:**
>
> $$W_{nc} = E_f - E_i$$
>
> According to your selections,
>
> $W_{nc} = 0$ (Conservative system: Mechanical energy is conserved)
>
> $E_f = (1/2)Mv^2$ and $E_i = Mgy$
>
> Please press any key to continue
>
> *****Work and Energy*****
>   1. Problem Solved
>   2. Return to Main Menu to continue solution
>   3. Review previous solution screens
>
> Please enter your selection: [1]
>
> **Fig. 3.2.** Sample problem and HAT menus needed to analyze problem.

Figure 3.2 shows a problem and the sequence of menus necessary to appropriately analyze the problem.

It is important to note that the menu-driven computer tool was not "smart" nor did it provide feedback on the appropriateness of the selections made to solve a problem. In fact, the tool (hence its "tool" designation) did not know what problem the student happened to be analyzing. It simply provided the opportunity to perform a conceptual analysis, which if correct, would reward the student with an equation that could be used to solve the problem. A user of the tool could (and often did) make incorrect menu selections during the analysis, in which case the tool would move to the next logical menu based on the previous menu selections. Hence, if the student made wrong choices, s/he would take an erroneous path that would not result in a correct equation at the end. The hope was that the student would, at some point during an incorrect analysis, recognize that the analysis was not going well, and back up to a previous menu, or start over with a new analysis (hence the options at the bottom of the menus that allowed students to back up or begin afresh, or to have a term defined in a glossary or to list all previous selections during the analysis).

In order to evaluate whether or not the tool made a difference, a control group participated in order to compare the focal treatment, where students analyzed/solved problems with the expert-like computer tool, with students who solved problems on their own without any aid. Thus the volunteers were divided into two groups, one focal group (the group that used the tool) and one control group. All students in the two groups solved the same 25 problems over five, one-hour treatment sessions (the other four sessions were used for testing).

To measure the impact of the treatments, two assessments were used, the first was a problem categorization task, the second a problem solving task. As reviewed earlier, novices tend to categorize problems according to surface attributes (e.g., the objects in the problem) whereas experts cue on the problems' deep structure (e.g., principles needed for solution) to categorize them. The expert-like tool asked in the first menu for the major principle needed to solve the problem, thus one would hypothesize that students using the tool for an extended period of time would be more likely to categorize problems according to principles compared to the other control treatment. Whether or not the problem solving measure would result in differential performance was an open question since all students practiced solving the same total number of problems in the two treatments.

Results of a study with the HAT tool showed that the treatment group attempted to categorize problems according to principles more often than the control group, and performed better on the problem solving assessment at the end of the study; both results were statistically significant. However, the accuracy of the students using the expert-like computer tool in terms of categorizing problems was not better than the control group. Hence, using the tool for 5 hours shifted students' categorization criteria towards using principles significantly more often than the control group but both groups were equally accurate in categorizing problems according to principles. This is not surprising since the ability to accurately categorize problems according to principles is a trait of expertise and, as reviewed above, it takes a long time to develop expertise—in other words, 5 hours is not enough to turn novices into expert categorizers, but 5 hours of practicing an expert-like analysis of problems did have an impact on novices' tendency to use principles in categorizing problems.

A more recent study (Docktor *et al.*, 2012) demonstrated that an even shorter intervention, lasting less than one hour, can impact novices' categorization criteria toward one that is principle-based. In that study, two groups of students enrolled in an introductory algebra-based mechanics course volunteered for the study two weeks prior to the end of the course (so that they had covered most of the material in the course). Students were divided into two groups consisting of a control and a focal treatment. In both treatments, students were presented with pairs of problems and asked "Would these problems be solved similarly?" and students would use a mouse to click "yes" or "no"; immediately upon answering yes or no, students were either given feedback on the appropriateness of their answer ("(In)Correct. These problems would (NOT) be solved similarly."), or asked to type into a text-box (free-form) the reasoning behind their answer; if prompted for reasoning, the feedback screen appeared immediately upon completing the typed explanation. Prompting for the reasoning that students used was done eight times during the one-hour experiment equally spaced throughout the experiment. Students in the control group were only told whether or not they were correct after answering yes/no to each problem pair. In contrast, the focal treatment, in addition, provided more elaborate feedback to the students, which included statements about the principle needed to solve the two problems. The control treatment will be referred to as the "sparse-feedback condition" while the focal treatment will be referred to as the "elaborate feedback condition." Figure 3.3 shows a sample item and the sequencing of screens as the experiment progressed. A total of 32 problem pairs were used that covered the major topics in the course.

The results in this study parallel the categorization results described in the previous study where students used the expert-like tool to analyze problems. Figure 3.4 shows the proportion of reasoning statements judged to be principle-based by two physics-expert-graders as a function of time as the experiment progressed (recall there were eight different occasions during which participants were asked to offer their reasoning equally spaced throughout the experiment). During the first half-hour of the experiment, reasoning statements based on physics principles hovered around 20–35%, with no significant differences between the sparse-feedback condition and the elaborate-feedback condition. However, there was a dramatic

Problem 1

While shopping you add a bag of dog food to your empty, stationary 14.5-kg cart. Then with a force of 12.0 N, you accelerate the cart at 0.6 m/s². What is the mass of the dog food?

Problem 2

A shopping cart of mass 30 kg is rolling along a level surface at a speed 0.5 m/s. A 2-kg carton of milk is dropped from rest and lands on the cart. What is the final speed of the cart and the milk?

Would these two problems be solved similarly?

Problem 1

While shopping you add a bag of dog food to your empty, stationary 14.5-kg cart. Then with a force of 12.0 N, you accelerate the cart at 0.6 m/s². What is the mass of the dog food?

Problem 2

A shopping cart of mass 30 kg is rolling along a level surface at a speed 0.5 m/s. A 2-kg carton of milk is dropped from rest and lands on the cart. What is the final speed of the cart and the milk?

Please explain the reason for your choice by typing in the box below.

Press the F1 key to continue.

(Continued)

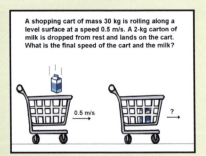

Fig. 3.3. Sample item used in categorization study. Reproduced from *Physical Review: Physics Education Research*, 2012, **8**(2), 020102 with permission from the American Physical Society.

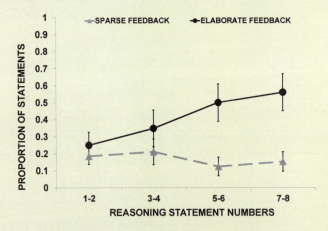

Fig. 3.4. Reasoning statements judged to be principle based as the experiment progressed. Reproduced from *Physical Review: Physics Education Research*, 2012, **8**(2), 020102 with permission from the American Physical Society.

shift during the second half-hour of the experiment, with students in the sparse-feedback condition lowering their use of principle-based reasoning to slightly more than 10% of the time, whereas the students in the elaborate-feedback condition employed principle-based reasoning more than 50% of the time. Thus it appears that even after one hour students can be influenced to use principle-based reasoning with feedback that mentions the principles used to solve problems. However, like in the previous study, there is also bad news here: Even though the students in the elaborate-feedback condition used principle-based reasoning significantly more often than students in the sparse-feedback group, the fraction of *correct* use of principles when using principle-based reasoning was equally poor for both groups; both groups were correct when using principle-based reasoning about 50% of the time. This and the previous study suggest that it is not difficult to steer students away from categorizing problems based on variable names or problems' surface attributes and more toward principle-based criteria—a good first step toward developing superior habits, but that it takes a much longer, sustained effort to help students use principle-based categorization *correctly*. Again, the latter finding is to be expected since if we were able to help students categorize problems accurately according to principles, which is a trait of expert physicists, with relative short interventions, then we would be able to turn novices into experts in short order, which is contrary to research into the development of expertise across all domains studied to date (e.g., chess, science, sports, …).

3.1.5.2. Longer-term interventions

Thus far the studies reviewed above indicate that it is relatively easy to influence novice students' behavior towards a more productive way of viewing physics as being comprised of a few major principles/concepts that can be applied to categorize and solve a wide range of problems, but their execution fell short, especially given the brief duration of the interventions. What if one could structure a study to promote a problem solving approach throughout an entire semester that allowed students to practice and receive feedback on a regimen where problems to be solved were first analyzed conceptually and then analyzed procedurally—might one see better execution of expert-like behaviors then? There are three examples of such studies, with all of them resulting in positive findings.

One study implemented "strategy writing" in an introductory calculus-based mechanics course (Leonard et al., 1996). Students were informed early in the semester that a strategy was a written paragraph with no equations that discussed the problem's solution at a high level and contained three components: (1) identification of the major principle(s) being applied, (2) a justification for why the principle(s) was applied to the particular problem under consideration, and (3) a procedure for applying the principle(s) to solve the problem (i.e., the *what*, *why* and *how* of solving a problem). Strategies were modeled for students in lecture— every time a sample problem was solved in lecture, the instructor began with a strategy, and then executed it to generate an answer. Strategies were also modeled in the posted written solutions to the weekly homework assignments (homework was neither collected nor graded), as well as by the instructors teaching the discussion sections whenever problems were solved. In order for students to take strategy writing seriously, all exams (75% multiple-choice and a "work-out" problem that was hand graded worth 25%) had one problem requiring a strategy and a solution, with 13 points assigned for the strategy and 12 for the executed solution.

Students, being very grade-conscious and wanting a lot of specificity, asked for more details about what a "good" strategy should look like, but the course instructors simply stated that there were many ways to write a strategy, and that as long as they discussed a coherent plan for solving a problem that contained the three elements it was fine; students were also told that a litmus test for a good strategy would be the following: If a student is stuck and does not know how to solve a problem, then handing them a good strategy would allow them to follow it to solve the problem. Figure 3.5 contains a strategy for a difficult two-principle problem from the posted solution to one of the homework sets. As one would expect, writing strategies was a struggle for students near the beginning of the course, but for most students, it steadily improved as the semester progressed.

Figure 3.6 shows a problem from the third midterm exam and sample student strategies, some good and some not-so-good. Note how the quality strategies contained the three components listed earlier, and displayed a coherent understanding of how to structure a problem's solution. On the other hand, it is difficult to "fake" a strategy—as can be seen, the below-average strategies were largely a "laundry list" of concepts and physics terms that lacked coherence and definitely did not pass the litmus test given earlier. By the end of the semester, about a third of the students could generate good strategies, about a third (those struggling in the course) were not able to put together a coherent strategy, and the middle third was somewhere in-between.

In addition to the work-out problem that was hand-graded in the exams that required a strategy, two additional measures were used to evaluate the semester-long impact of writing strategies. One was a problem categorization task consisting of 5 multiple-choice problems given as part of the final exam.

Problem:
A stick of mass M and length L is hanging from a ceiling as shown to the right. A piece of putty of mass m is traveling horizontally when it strikes and adheres to the stick at its midpoint. What must have been the speed of the putty, v, if the stick (with putty attached) swings and comes momentarily to rest in a horizontal position before starting to swing down again?

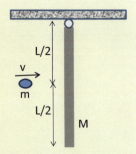

Strategy:
This problem consists of two parts. First, the mass and stick undergo a totally inelastic collision. Angular momentum is conserved about the pivot during the collision since there is no net external torque (about the pivot). Even though there are two external forces present during the collision, these do not provide a net external torque: The force at the pivot has no moment arm (i.e., r = 0) and so it does not provide a torque about the pivot. The gravitational force acting on the center of mass of the stick points vertically down and initially is parallel to r (i.e., angle between r and F_g is 0). Assuming the collision is instantaneous, the gravitational force delivers no angular impulse to the system during the collision. So, assuming there is no friction between the pivot and the rod, there are no angular impulses delivered to the putty-stick system. Thus, for the collision portion of the problem, equate the initial and the final angular momenta of the putty-stick system. Note that only the putty contributes to the initial angular momentum since the stick is at rest prior to the collision.

The second part of the problem consists of the putty-stick system rotating to a horizontal position before momentarily stopping. During this portion of the problem, mechanical energy is conserved. Only two forces act on the system during this "swinging" portion: The gravitational force and the force at the pivot. The force at the pivot does no work since the pivot point does not move and we have assumed that there is no friction between the pivot and the stick. Only the gravitational force (a conservative force) does work, resulting in mechanical energy being conserved. Thus, for the second portion of the problem, equate the initial and the final mechanical energies of the system. Assuming the collision was instantaneous, the initial orientation of the putty-stick system is vertical. The center of mass of the system is at the midpoint of the stick. (We need this to evaluate the potential energy of the system.) Applying the two concepts of angular momentum and energy conservation will result in two equations that will allow you to solve for v in terms of the "givens" in the problem.

Fig. 3.5. Sample problem and strategy from posted homework solutions. Reproduced from *American Journal of Physics*, **64**, 1495–1503 with permission.

Problem:
A disk of mass, M = 2 kg, and radius, R = 0.4 m, has string wound around it and is free to rotate about an axle through its center. A block of mass, m = 1 kg, is attached to the end of the string and the system is released from rest with no slack in the string. What is the speed of the block after it has fallen a distance, d = 0.5 m. Don't forget to provide both a strategy and a solution.

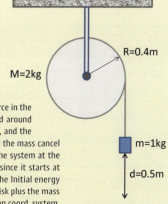

Above Average Strategies:
A1: Use the Conservation of Energy since the only non-conservative force in the system is the tension in the rope attached to the mass M and wound around the disk, (assuming there is no friction between the axle and the disk, and the mass M and the air), and the work done by the tension to the disk and the mass cancel each other out. First set up a coord. syst. so the potential energy of the system at the start can be determined. There will be no kinetic energy at the start since it starts at rest. Therefore the potential energy is all the initial energy. Now set the Initial energy equal to the final energy that is made up of the kinetic energy of the disk plus the mass m and any potential energy left in the system with respect to the chosen coord. system.

A2: I would use conservation of mechanical energy to solve this problem. The mass m has some potential energy while it is hanging there. When the block starts to accelerate downwards the potential energy is transformed into rotational Kinetic energy of the disk and Kinetic energy of the falling mass. Equating the initial and final states; and using the relationship between v and w the speed of m can be found. Mechanical energy is conserved even with the non-conservative Tension force because the Tension force is internal to the system. (pulley, mass, rope)

A3: The linear velocity is related to the angular velocity by the factor of the disc's radius. In this problem, the pivot is frictionless so all energy is conserved. By equating the initial energy (potential of hanging mass) with the final energy (kinetic of mass & kinetic of rotating disc), it is then possible, after changing the rotational velocity to its linear form, to isolate and calculate a value for the final linear velocity.

A4: Apply Newton Second Law to find the net force acting on the block. This is equal to its mass times its acceleration. This net force, crossed with the radius of the disk, provides a net torque. The net torque is the moment of inertia of the disk times the angular acceleration. Solve both equations for the accelerations. They are related because the acceleration is the cross product of the radius and the angular acceleration. Substitute what you solved for in the two equations above, and then solve for Tension (T). Substitute this for T in the equation for acceleration and then solve using math.

Below Average Strategies:
B1: Using d = 0.5 m, we could find θ and from there we could figure out the time using θ, a, and ω_0. After we found this, we could use that, along with the other given information to determine the angular speed. Once we know this, we can relate the angular information to the block.

B2: Not only do you have to consider the mass of the block on the string but also the force of gravity on the block. Rotational kinematics must be used with the radius, mass and gravity.

B3: In trying to find the speed of the block I would try to find angular momentum kinetic energy, use gravity, I would also use rotational kinematics and Moment of Inertia around the center of mass for the disk.

B4: There will be a torque about the center of mass due to the weight of the block, m. The force pulling downward is mg. The moment of inertia about the axle is 1/2 MR2. The moment of inertia multiplied by the angular acceleration. By plugging these values into a kinematic expression, the angular speed can be calculated. Then, the angular speed times the radius gives you the velocity of the block.

Fig. 3.6. Sample student strategies from mid-term exam. (The strategies above are transcribed verbatim from students' exam papers). Reproduced from *American Journal of Physics*, **64**, 1495–1503 with permission.

Below are five choices labeled a-e containing one or more major concepts studied in the course. Questions 1-5 consist of five problems that you do not need to solve. Your job is to decide which major concept(s) needs to be applied to solve each problem in the most efficient manner and make the appropriate selection. Use the same set of five multiple choices for all five questions, and you may use each choice, A-E, once, more than once, or not at all.

Multiple Choices:

(A) Newton's Second Law
(B) Work-Energy Theorem or Conservation of Mechanical Energy
(C) Linear Momentum or Conservation of Linear Momentum
(D) Conservation of Linear Momentum followed by Conservation of Mechanical Energy
(E) Angular Momentum or Conservation of Angular Momentum

Problems:

1. A 2 kg uniform metal bar of length 1 m resting on a frictionless horizontal surface is free to rotate about a pivot at one end. A 5 g bullet traveling perpendicular to the stick hits and embeds itself into the stick 50 cm from the pivot. If the initial speed of the bullet is 300 m/s, what is the angular speed of the stick immediately following the collision.

2. A mass M is connected to a string of length L to form a simple pendulum, with the other end of the string attached to the ceiling. The pendulum is released from rest at height L/2 from the lowest point of the pendulum's swing. What is the speed of the mass at the lowest point in the swing? Consider the string to be massless.

3. A block of mass m is moving at speed v along a horizontal, frictionless surface. The block undergoes a perfectly inelastic collision with a second block of mass M. The two blocks proceed up a frictionless inclined plane and momentarily come to rest part way up the plane. What maximum distance along the inclined plane do the two blocks travel?

4. A 1 kg stick of length 2 m is placed on a frictionless surface and is free to rotate about a vertical pivot through one end. A 50 g lump of putty is attached 80 cm from the pivot. What is the magnitude of the force between the stick and the putty when the angular velocity of the system is 3 rad/s?

5. A mass M is connected to a string of length L to form a simple pendulum, with the other end of the string attached to the ceiling. If the mass has speed v at the bottom of the swing, what is the tension in the rope at that point? Consider the string to be massless.

Fig. 3.7. Categorization task.
(The five multiple choice questions were administered as part of the final exam). Reproduced from *American Journal of Physics*, **64**, 1495–1503 with permission.

Each question asked students to read a problem and then to select from among five multiple choices the major principle(s) that should be applied to solve the problem in the most efficient way possible (students were not required to solve those five problems). The five questions are listed in Fig. 3.7. Because the first component of a strategy was identifying the principle(s) needed to solve a problem, it was expected that the strategy writing class would do better on these five problems compared to students in the same course, a semester later, that was taught traditionally without strategy writing. Averaging over the five questions, the traditional class selected the correct principle 48% of the time whereas the strategy writing class did so 70% of the time (more details are provided in (Leonard et al., 1996).

The last measure used probed students' memories about the most important physics ideas covered in the course months after taking it. Since there was likely to be substantial forgetting as time passed, the researchers decided only to probe students who had gotten a very high grade, hence volunteers were sought who had earned grades in the A range. Because the two courses were taught in different semesters, students from the traditional class had finished the course six months prior, while the strategy writing students had finished the course eleven months prior. Students were asked to name/write down the most important physics ideas used to solve problems in mechanics. Students generally identified seven principles, namely Newton's three laws, conservation of energy, momentum, and angular momentum, and the work-energy theorem. Both groups identified Newton's three laws with about the same frequency. However, the strategy writing students mentioned the other four principles beyond Newton's Laws at a much higher rate than the traditionally taught students, with 92% mentioning one principle beyond

Newton's Laws compared to 36% for the traditional class, and 69% mentioning two principles beyond Newton's Laws compared to 9% for the traditional class. Note that this does not mean that one group was better, or less able than the other group in solving problems since students were not tested for problem solving skills months after the course was over, nor that the strategy students had a better conceptual understanding of the material since that was also not tested. However, focusing on a regimen that consistently forces students to consider principles in problem solving does impact their ability to recall and name the major principles covered in the course months after it was over.

A second study by Van Heuvelen (1991a, 1991b) used an approach to teach mechanics called *Overview, Case Study Physics (OCS)*. The approach was used in a large lecture course and required two passes through the material. In the first pass, which lasted about one-third of the semester, students were exposed to the entire course content qualitatively, actively discussing concepts, representing them in diagram form and confronting erroneous preconceptions. Students also worked on qualitative problems during lecture in groups, and at the end of the first third of the course, they were tested with an exam consisting of qualitative questions about the entire course content. In the second two-thirds of the course, the same material is revisited but now in mathematical form where they solve quantitative problems applying the concepts they learned previously. Students were also provided with a flow chart with a hierarchical representation of the concepts in the course (e.g., starting at the top with dynamics and conserved motion) and naming the major concepts both in words and equation form. Students were assigned complicated, multi-concept problems to solve in groups where they were required to integrate and apply the concepts learned in the course and generate a numerical solution. In assessments given at the end of the semester, the OCS students (in both algebra-based and calculus-based mechanics) outperformed traditionally taught classes in both conceptual questions and in problem solving. As in the strategy writing study, the OCS approach also resulted in better retention. One month after finishing a traditional mechanics course and eight months after finishing an OCS course, students were given a qualitative, conceptual diagnostic test where the OCS students scored 20% higher than the traditional students (despite the much longer period of time over which OCS students could have "forgotten" the material).

The third investigation consisted of a series of classroom-based studies conducted over a number of years by Gautreau and Novemsky (1997). Those studies attempted to adopt/replicate the OCS approach by a faculty member who had not been involved in the development of the OCS method. OCS was used in teaching various courses to both mainstream students as well as minority students enrolled in an Educational Opportunity Program (EOP) with end-of-course exam performance compared to students taking the same course taught traditionally. In all cases that compared the performance of OCS-students with traditionally-taught students, the OCS students significantly outperformed traditionally-taught students in both conceptual and problem solving measures. In fact, EOP students who had experienced the OCS approach also outperformed the traditionally-taught mainstream students.

3.2. What are the implications of expert–novice research for instruction?

We offer the following implications of the research reviewed above for instruction:

- **Developing expertise in any endeavor, including a complex domain such as physics, takes considerable time and effort.** Because the development of expertise takes a long time, we cannot expect beginning students to possess a well-organized memory store of physics concepts and problem solving procedures (although perhaps the most advanced beginning students will be on their way to developing them). Lacking an expert's perspective, novices approach problem solving in the best way they can, which largely consists of matching the variables in a problem to equations containing those variables. Students would not try this method if it did not have some merit—a lot of times, finding relevant equations and manipulating them will work in finding a solution to a problem. Students also tend to work by analogy, matching problems they are solving to similar-looking problems they have solved before or worked out problems in textbooks. However, matching problems on surface attributes can lead to erroneous solutions since different concepts are often used to solve similar-looking problems.
- **As instructors, it is important to be aware that students notice different things in physics situations than we do.** Experts possess considerable tacit knowledge, much of which is not exposed to students during our teaching. Experts' knowledge allows them to "see" subtle features in physics situations that help develop a deep understanding of the situation. Novices are not so privileged, and often miss things in physics situations that we as experts consider obvious (recall the expert's blind spot discussed in Chapter 1).
- **Research studies show promise for helping beginning students adopt traits of experts in problem solving and**

conceptual development. Although progression toward expertise is slow, it can be made more efficient. Since beginning students are adept at algebraic manipulations of equations, that is their go-to method for solving problems. Focusing on conceptual aspects of problem solving, such as beginning to solve a problem by considering what concepts/principles apply, is not something beginning physics students typically do. However, research indicates that interventions can be developed to help students elevate the role of concepts in problem solving and consider what concepts/principles can be applied to solve problems. The only caveat is that getting novices to consider concepts is not equivalent to having them consider *appropriate* concepts for a given problem—that skill takes much longer to develop.

3.3. Examples of teaching interventions based on learning research

The research reviewed in this chapter suggests that introductory students could benefit from three types of instructional strategies that are typically absent in traditional instruction: (1) Elevating the role of concepts/principles in problem solving, (2) Organizing physics knowledge more efficiently in memory, and (3) Making the tacit knowledge that experts use in problem solving explicit during instruction. Below we provide some instructional suggestions for implementing these strategies during the normal course of instruction; with the suggestions below, we are not advocating wholesale change in teaching practices but rather the integration of some new practices and activities in homework and in-class practices. If you decide to implement some of the instructional suggestions below, it is important that students take the task seriously, and unfortunately the only way to do so is to count it as part of the students' course grade. Note how the suggestions below are largely qualitative and not quantitative.

Instructional strategies to elevate the role of concepts/principles in problem solving:

- **Implement problem categorization.** Problem categorization is an activity that offers fruitful opportunities for blending conceptual knowledge with problem solving. Categorizing problems according to the major concept/principle needed for solving them is less time-consuming than actually solving problems, thus one can go through many more practice items in the same time than it would take to solve just a few problems. Categorization also offers the opportunity to compare/contrast the usefulness of seeking a problem's underlying conceptual structure for strategizing a solution, as opposed to simply focusing on surface attributes such as objects or variables in the problem. Unfortunately, this task needs to wait until several major principles are covered in a course (likely mid-way through a course and beyond) because it would be rather pointless to give items that all require the same major principle for solution.

Problem categorization tasks can take various forms, each with its own nuance (Hardiman et al., 1989). For example, giving pairs of problems and asking if they are solved similarly together with providing a justification allows one to draw attention to extracting the deep structure from the problems' surface attributes. The "answer" to a two-problem categorization task, as seen previously, is binary: The two problems are either solved similarly (i.e., by applying the same principle) or not. But the problem pair

The following pair of problems match on surface features but not deep structure

Two blocks of mass 10 kg and 8 kg are connected by a light compressed spring of force constant 80 N/m and held at rest. The blocks are released and the 10 kg block is observed to move at 2 m1sec. Find the velocity of the 8 kg block.

A 15 kg block and a 10 kg block are connected by a light compressed spring of force constant 200 N/m and held at rest. The blocks are released and observed to move at 2 m/s and 3 m/s respectively in opposite directions. Find the distance the spring was compressed from its equilibrium length.

The following pair of problems match on deep structure but not on surface features

Two blocks of mass 10 kg and 8 kg are connected by a light compressed spring of force constant 80 N/m and held at rest. The blocks are released and the 10 kg block is observed to move at 2 m1sec. Find the velocity of the 8 kg block.

A bullet of mass 10 g is fired into a target of mass 10 kg. The bullet and target then have a common velocity of 1 m/s. How fast was the bullet moving just before it entered the target?

Fig. 3.8. Two-problem categorization task.

could also match on surface attributes, or not. If done as a class activity, the instructor could draw attention to how one extracts the deep structure from problems (valuable tacit knowledge) and warn students against their tendency to think that problems that look alike are solved similarly. Two examples of a two-problem categorization task are shown in Fig. 3.8, where in the first pair the problems match on surface features but not on deep structure (thus they are not solved similarly), and in the second pair the problems match on deep structure but not on surface features.

Another form of a problem categorization task is a three-problem format, as shown in Fig. 3.9 (for many more items see (Hardiman et al., 1989)). Here one gives a "model problem" and two "comparison problems" and the student's job is to determine which of the two comparison problems is solved similarly to the model problem. One can be more methodical with

Model Problem: Two blocks of mass 10 kg and 8 kg are connected by a light compressed spring of force constant 80 N/m and held at rest. The blocks are released and the 10 kg block is observed to move at 2 m/s. Find the velocity of the 8 kg block.

S Comparison Problem: A 15 kg block and a 10 kg block are connected by a light compressed spring of force constant 200 N/m and held at rest. The blocks are released and observed o move at 2 m/s and 3 m/s respectively in opposite directions. Find the distance the spring was compressed from its equilibrium length.

D Comparison Problem: A bullet of mass 10 g is fired into a target of mass 10 kg. The bullet and target then have a common velocity of 1 m/s. How fast was the bullet moving just before it entered the target?

SD Comparison Problem: Two blocks each of mass 20 kg are connected by a light, compressed spring of force constant 70 N/m. After the blocks are released, it is observed that one of the blocks has received an impulse of magnitude 150 N/sec. Find the speed of the other block.

N Comparison Problem: A 10 kg mass with initial velocity 2 m1sec passes over a rough horizontal surface with a coefficient of kinetic friction 0.1. Find the acceleration of the mass when it is on the rough surface.

Fig. 3.9. To form a three-problem categorization item, use the Model Problem and the following two Comparison Problem combinations: S-D, S-SD, N-D, N-SD. The task for the student is to determine which Comparison Problem is solved most like the Model Problem.

this format in drawing contrasts between surface attributes and concepts/principles needed for solution. Clearly one (and only one) of the two comparison problems would need to match the model problem on deep structure (the same concept(s)/principle(s) would be applied to solve both) for there to be a unique correct answer, but problems in the pair could be of four types: (1) No match (N), meaning that a comparison problem does not match the model problem on either surface attributes or deep structure, (2) Match on surface features only (S), meaning that a comparison problem matches the model problem only on surface attributes, (3) Match on deep structure only (D), meaning that a comparison problem matches the model problem only on the concept(s)/principle(s) needed for solution, and (4) Match on both surface attributes and deep structure (SD). Thus, the pair of comparison problems could have one of the following four forms: S-D, S-SD, N-D and N-SD. For students who exhibit standard novice behavior, the hardest type of item would be S-D since they would be tempted to match on surface attributes, and the easiest would be N-SD since matching on either surface feature or deep structure would result in a correct answer. This type of task could be assigned for homework, for an in-class collaborative activity with the instructor providing coaching, or in discussion section as a group activity that is then discussed in class-wide format.

A third form would be a multiple choice format as discussed earlier (see Fig. 3.7), where a problem would be given together with multiple choices for the principle(s) needed to solve the problem. The student would attempt to choose the correct principle(s) needed for solving the problem. This format lends itself well for web-based homework formats or for multiple choice exams.

In summary, problem categorization is an efficient way to expose students to the role that concepts and principles play in solving problems, and in addition, offers the instructor opportunities to discuss the procedures for applying the major concepts/principles, thereby revealing valuable tacit knowledge.

- **Implement strategy writing.** The classroom-based study described above (Leonard *et al.*, 1996) where students wrote strategies for solving problems before solving them is an excellent task for both, blending all the crucial aspects of problem solving, and for revealing to students the tacit knowledge that experts use in solving problems.

As we have defined it, the three components of a strategy consist of identifying the major principle(s) needed to solve the problem, justifying why the principle applies, and describing a procedure in words for applying the principle. In short, a strategy is a prose description of how to go about solving a problem. A couple of caveats are in order. First, strategy writing is a high level task that students will find difficult to do (at least initially), so modeling it for students is important. Also, since it is so unlike the typical tasks assigned in physics courses, be prepared for students resisting and offering gratuitous commentary such as "writing belongs in English class." Motivating students is important for them to invest in an activity, so telling them the purpose of strategy writing is important.

Note what strategy writing accomplishes that not only is crucial for problem solving training, but that also is not typically done in traditional instruction. First, it is a top-down approach for solving problems, starting with identifying the principle(s) that can be applied to solve a problem, as opposed to starting with equation manipulation. The second component of a strategy also reveals valuable tacit knowledge that typically remains hidden during instruction, namely deciding the conditions under which a particular principle can be applied. For example, during the course of instruction we might work out a problem for students and state that we are applying conservation of mechanical energy and move directly to the equation that sets the mechanical energy in the initial state to the mechanical energy in the final state. Doing so sweeps under the rug how we as experts decided that conservation of mechanical energy could be applied to the situation, namely the absence of work done by non-conservative forces. Checking for conditions of applicability is an expert trait that students would find useful to learn early on. The third component, describing a procedure for applying the principle(s) to solve the problem also elevates procedural knowledge in ways that are generalizable. If all beginning students do is work at the equation-manipulation level, it is hard for them to pull out the meaning underlying the equations they use. Describing a procedure in words reveals the structure of the solution and provides opportunities for generalizability. For example, the procedure for applying conservation laws in mechanics is exactly the same whether we do it for mechanical energy, momentum or angular momentum; the only thing that changes is whether the equation used has variables E, P or L.

One way to ease students into strategies for solving problems is to provide them with a strategy (written by the instructor) and have students execute it to solve the problem. This would be a considerably easier task than writing actual strategies, and it allows students to interpret a strategy and follow it as a high-level recipe for solving a problem. Note that providing students with strategies to execute allows instructors to assign difficult problems that might otherwise be very time-consuming for students. For example, two-principle problems, such as the problem shown in Fig. 3.5, are known to be harder for students than single-principle problems, but with a recipe to follow, students are much more likely to make rapid progress toward a solution.

Another approach to strategy writing is to provide much more scaffolding to help students focus on the elements of a strategy and then as they become proficient the instructor can gradually fade the supports (Docktor *et al.*, 2015). One example of how to provide scaffolding is to use the format shown in Fig. 3.10, where a strategy is broken down into the principle, justification and plan (all clearly labeled), and then the plan is

> A skateboarder enters a curved ramp moving horizontally with a speed of 6.5 m/s, and leaves the ramp moving vertically with a speed of 4.1 m/s. The skateboarder and the skateboard have a combined mass of 55 kg. Find the height of the ramp, assuming no energy loss to frictional forces.

Principle:
Conservation of energy: the total mechanical energy (sum of kinetic and potential energies) of an isolated system is the same in the initial and final states.

Justification:
Mechanical energy is conserved if there are no non-conservative forces that do not work on the system. The normal force exerted on the skateboarder is a non-conservative force, but the work that the normal force does is 0 because its direction is always perpendicular to the displacement. The gravitational force is conservative (it is already included in the potential energy term), and we are ignoring non-conservative frictional forces. Therefore, mechanical energy is conserved.

Plan:
1. Draw a picture and assign symbols for quantities in the problem. Choose a coordinate system.
2. Write an equation for conservation of mechanical energy. Expand the equation to include the initial and final kinetic and potential energy terms.
3. Solve for the height of the ramp. Substitute values to get an answer.

Two-Column Solution:

Plan Step	Equation(s) used in step
1. Draw a picture and assign symbols for quantities in the problem. Choose a coordinate system.	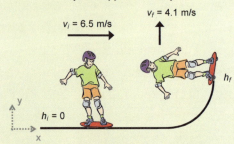
	$m = 55$ kg — Mass of the skateboarder and skateboard combined
	$v_i = 6.5$ m/s — Initial speed of skateboarder
	$v_f = 4.1$ m/s — Final speed of skateboarder
	$h_i = 0$ m — Initial height of skateboarder

(Continued)

2. Write an equation for conservation of mechanical energy. Expand this equation to include the initial and final kinetic and potential energy terms.

$$\Delta E = 0 \Rightarrow E_i = E_f$$

$$KE_i + PE_i = KE_f + PE_f$$

$$\tfrac{1}{2}mv_i^2 + mgh_i = \tfrac{1}{2}mv_f^2 + mgh_f$$

$$\tfrac{1}{2}mv_i^2 + 0 = \tfrac{1}{2}mv_f^2 + mgh_f$$

3. Solve for the height of the ramp. Substitute values to get an answer.

$$mgh_f = \tfrac{1}{2}mv_f^2 - \tfrac{1}{2}mv_i^2$$

$$h_f = \frac{\tfrac{1}{2}\cancel{m}v_f^2 - \tfrac{1}{2}\cancel{m}v_i^2}{\cancel{m}g}$$

$$h_f = \frac{\tfrac{1}{2}v_f^2 - \tfrac{1}{2}v_i^2}{g}$$

$$= \frac{\tfrac{1}{2}(4.1 \text{ m/s})^2 - \tfrac{1}{2}(6.5 \text{ m/s})^2}{(9.8 \text{ m/s}^2)}$$

$$= 1.3 m$$

Fig. 3.10. Scaffolding for problem-solving strategies.

executed using a two-column solution. Using this format, students would be provided with a partially-filled "worksheet" (as in Fig. 3.10) and task students to work collaboratively to complete the worksheet.

- **Implement assessments that promote conceptual understanding.** Chapter 2 provided an overview of active learning strategies to promote conceptual understanding. Another suggestion we offer called "finding errors" consists of a task whereby a problem is given together with a solution consisting of a brief conceptual analysis of the problem followed by a solution. The conceptual analysis and solution contain a conceptual error that results in an incorrect solution to the problem. The error is subtle and draws on typical student misconceptions. Figure 3.11 provides an example. The error here, consisting of the common student misconception (Feil & Mestre, 2010; McDermott et al., 1994; Mestre, 2002) that the tension in the string is equal to the weight of the hanging mass, has been observed by many of us in teaching introductory mechanics.

We need to point out several caveats about this task. Because this task draws on common misconceptions and/or student errors,

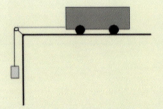

A block of mass 0.25 kg is connected to a cart of mass 0.75 kg by a string and a frictionless pulley, as shown in the figure below. There is no friction as the cart is rolling on the horizontal track. What is the acceleration of the cart?

Solution:

We can use Newton's 2nd Law to find the acceleration of the cart. The net force on the cart will equal the cart's mass multiplied by its acceleration. The tension in the string is equal to the weight of the hanging block. The net force on the cart is equal to the tension in the string because the force of gravity on the cart and the normal force on the cart cancel each other out. The mass of the cart is given (0.75 kg), so we can find the acceleration of the cart.

$$F_{net} = m_{cart} a$$

$$T = m_{cart} a$$

$$a = \frac{T}{m_{cart}}$$

$$T = m_{block} g$$

$$a = \frac{m_{block} g}{m_{cart}}$$

$$a = \frac{(0.25 \text{ kg})(9.81 \text{ m/s}^2)}{0.75 \text{ kg}}$$

$$a = 3.27 \text{ m/s}^2$$

Explain what is wrong with this solution and why it is incorrect.

Fig. 3.11. Identifying conceptual errors in solutions.

it is a high-level, difficult task. We used it in a high school classroom physics study evaluating innovative teaching strategies (Docktor *et al.*, 2015) as an end-of-course assessment and found that the performance was at floor-levels (students averaged 6% in an assessment comprised of items like the one above). Also, as far as we know this type of exercise has not been tried at the college level, although we would predict that the performance would be higher than that at the high school level. In developing items like that in Fig. 3.11, care should be taken so that the error in the solution is not outrageous and easily identifiable—the error should be plausible so that it "blends in" to the solution.

Instructional strategies to help students develop a hierarchical structure of physics:

- **Implement concept map diagrams or flow charts**. The Van Heuvelen (1991a, 1991b) classroom study reviewed earlier used a hierarchical flow chart to reveal the structure of the physics course. There is no single "correct" flow chart, although there should be substantial overlap in the flow charts generated by different instructors. Such a flow chart can be generated and filled in as the course progresses in order to help students organize their physics knowledge efficiently. Typically the hierarchy will show the major principles at the top, and under each principle how different conditions lead to specific forms of the major principle (e.g., under work and energy, would be such branches as work done by conservative and non-conservative forces, potential and kinetic energies, the work-energy theorem and conservation of mechanical energy). As one looks down the hierarchy, the entries become more specific, for example, discussing procedures and equations for applying the concepts.

As reviewed earlier, novices find it difficult to "see" the structure of a discipline until they gain considerable experience; however, that does not mean that novices cannot be assisted in building a more expert-like structure in memory of the subject matter. Textbooks do not help to reveal the hierarchy of physics, and students tend to view content coverage in lectures and textbooks as a linear journey through unrelated topics. Building a hierarchical flow chart and using it to think about solutions to problems is one way of helping novices begin to restructure their amorphous memory store of physics ideas into a more coherent whole. How to "count" such a flow chart in a course's grading structure so that students take it seriously is a bit trickier. One approach is to ask students to take problems they have previously solved and trace the path of the solution through the hierarchy. Such an exercise would need to take place during the last half of the course when a substantial portion of the flow chart has been filled in or the exercise becomes rather trivial (i.e., all kinematic problems follow the same path more or less).

There has been some research on implementing "link maps" in introductory physics courses to illustrate the key concepts from lecture and how they are related to each other (Lindstrøm & Sharma, 2009, 2011). In those studies, the instructor provided a map of concepts and modeled how to use it during optional problem solving "map meetings." Students who attended the map meetings had higher retention, more positive feedback about the course, and scored higher on exams. The strategy was particularly effective for low-achieving students.

- **Highlight connections in the course content.** As an instructor, you might already highlight for your students how the content builds or is an extension of what they've learned previously. For example, if students in an electricity and magnetism class are starting to learn about electric forces between charged particles, you might remind them how they previously solved force problems when they learned about Newton's laws of motion in mechanics (breaking force vectors into components, analyzing the sum of the forces along each coordinate axis, etc.). Or, instead of pointing out these connections, you might elicit students' existing knowledge on a topic and help them make their own connections.

Instructional strategies for making tacit knowledge explicit:

- **Justify problem-solving decisions.** As an expert on routine physics problems or "exercises" in your view, it can be easy to go into autopilot mode when writing down a problem solution. It is important to remember that many of your decisions have become automatic and you do not even have to think about what comes next, but for a novice this is a common struggle. It is valuable for beginning students to see every procedure unpacked and explained. When modeling how to solve an example problem for your students, start from the very beginning and explicitly discuss the justifications for each step. In addition, practice steps that will benefit students—before writing equations, start by representing the information given in the problem (such as with a picture, diagram, and assigning symbols for quantities). Then explain how you use that given information to decide on an approach with the basic physics concepts and principles. Highlight the conditions under which those concepts and principles are applicable (see strategy writing above). Show all steps in writing specific equations and arithmetic to reach an answer, even if it seems trivial. Model how you evaluate whether the answer makes sense. Recall that a novice has to practice making deliberate decisions before they can become an advanced beginner or competent problem solver.

- **Implement principle identification exercises.** Experts tacitly consider which principle(s) apply to problems and then apply it(them) in equation form to solve them. Novices tend to skip the principle identification stage and go straight to equation manipulation. Exercises where students are presented with problems, one at a time, and asked to identify the principle needed for solution (without actually solving the problem) would make this type of tacit knowledge visible for students. Note that this is the first step in strategy writing, however, the additional two steps in strategy writing (justifying the principle and describing a procedure for solving the problem) are rather time consuming. Having only principle identification would allow many problems to be considered in a short time span and offer the instructor opportunities for discussing with students how to extract the needed principle from the problem's surface attributes.

In Chapter 4 we will highlight additional instructional strategies appropriate for teaching problem solving.

References

Chi, M.T.H. (2006). Two approaches to the study of experts' characteristics. In K.A. Ericsson, N. Charness, R.R. Hoffman & P.J. Feltovich (Eds.), *The Cambridge Handbook of Expertise and Expert Performance*, pp. 21–30. New York, NY: Cambridge University Press.

Chi, M.T.H., Feltovich, P.J. & Glaser, R. (1981). Categorization and representation of physics problems by experts and novices. *Cognitive Science*, **5**, 121–152.

Docktor, J.L, Mestre, J.P. & Ross, B.H. (2012). Impact of a short intervention on novices' categorization criteria. *Physical Review Special Topics – Physics Education Research*, **8**(020102), 1–11. https://doi.org/10.1103/PhysRevSTPER.8.020102

Docktor, J.L., Strand, N.E., Mestre, J.P. & Ross, B.H. (2015). Conceptual problem solving in high school physics. *Physical Review Special Topics – Physics Education Research*, **11**(020106), 1–13. https://doi.org/10.1103/PhysRevSTPER.11.020106

Dreyfus, H.L. & Dreyfus, S.E. (1986). *Mind Over Machine: The Power of Human Intuition And Expertise In An Era Of The Computer*. New York: Free Press.

Dufresne, R., Gerace, W.J., Hardiman, P.T. & Mestre, J.P. (1992). Constraining novices to perform expert-like problem analyses: Effects on schema acquisition. *Journal of the Learning Sciences*, **2**, 307–331. https://doi.org/10.1207/s15327809jls0203_3

Ericsson, K.A., Krampe, R.Th. & Tesch-Romer, C. (1993). The role of deliberate practice in the acquisition of expert performance. *Psychological Review*, **100**, 393–394.

Feil, A. & Mestre, J.P. (2010). Change blindness as a means of studying expertise in physics. *Journal of the Learning Sciences*, **19**(4), 480–505.

Gautreau, R. & Novemsky, L. (1997). Concepts first—A small group approach to physics learning. *American Journal of Physics*, **65**, 418–428.

Gick, M.L. (1986). Problem-solving strategies. *Educational Psychologist*, **21**(1&2), 99–120. https://doi.org/10.1080/00461520.1986.9653026

Hardiman, P.T., Dufresne, R. & Mestre, J.P. (1989). The relation between problem categorization and problem solving among novices and experts. *Memory & Cognition*, **17**, 627–638.

Larkin, J.H., McDermott, J., Simon, D.P. & Simon, H.A. (1980). Models of competence in solving physics problems. *Cognitive Science*, **4**, 317–345.

Leonard, W.J., Dufresne, R.J. & Mestre, J.P. (1996). Using qualitative problem-solving strategies to highlight the role of conceptual knowledge in solving problems. *American Journal of Physics*, **64**(12), 1495–1503.

Lindstrøm, C. & Sharma, M.D. (2009). Link maps and map meetings: Scaffolding student learning. *Physical Review Special Topics – Physics Education Research*, **5**(010102), 1–11. https://doi.org/10.1103/PhysRevSTPER.5.010102

Lindstrøm, C. & Sharma, M.D. (2011). Teaching physics novices at university: A case for stronger scaffolding. *Physical Review Special Topics – Physics Education Research*, **7**(010109), 1–14. https://doi.org/10.1103/PhysRevSTPER.7.010109

Madsen, A.M., Larson, A.M., Loschky, L.C. & Rebello, N.S. (2012). Differences in visual attention between those who correctly and incorrectly answer physics problems. *Physical Review Special Topics – Physics Education Research*, **8**(010122), 1–13. https://doi.org/10.1103/PhysRevSTPER.8.010122

McDermott, L.C., Shaffer, P.S. & Sommers, M.D. (1994). Research as a guide for teaching introductory mechanics: An illustration in the context of the Atwood's Machine. *American Journal of Physics*, **62**, 46–55.

Mestre, J. (2002). Probing adults' conceptual understanding and transfer of learning via problem posing. *Journal of Applied Developmental Psychology*, **23**, 9–50.

National Research Council (2000). *How People Learn: Brain, Mind, Experience, and School: Expanded Edition*. Washington, DC: The National Academies Press. https://doi.org/10.17226/9853

Reif., F. & Heller, J.I. (1982). Knowledge structure and problem solving in physics. *Educational Psychologist*, **17**(2), 102–127. https://doi.org/10.1080/00461528209529248

Sweller, J. (2011). Cognitive load theory. In J. P. Mestre & B. H. Ross (Eds.), *The Psychology of Learning and Motivation: Cognition in Education*, Vol. 55, pp. 37–76. San Diego, CA, US: Elsevier Academic Press. http://dx.doi.org/10.1016/B978-0-12-387691-1.00002-8

Van Heuvelen, A. (1991a). Learning to think like a physicist: A review of research-based instructional strategies. *American Journal of Physics*, **59**(10), 891–897. https://doi.org/10.1119/1.16667

Van Heuvelen, A. (1991b). Overview, case study physics. *American Journal of Physics*, **59**(10), 898–907. https://doi.org/10.1119/1.16668

Van Heuvelen, A. & Maloney. D. (1999). Playing physics jeopardy. *American Journal of Physics*, **67**(3), 252–256. https://doi.org/10.1119/1.19233

Walsh, L.N., Howard, R.G. & Bowe, B. (2007). Phenomenographic study of students' problem solving approaches in physics. *Physical Review Special Topics – Physics Education Research*, **3**(020108), 1–12. https://doi.org/10.1103/PhysRevSTPER.3.020108

Chapter

4. From Manipulating Equations to a More Conceptual Approach:
How to Improve Problem Solving

4.1. What does research on problem solving tell us?

We have all witnessed that, when solving physics problems, beginning physics students focus on searching for equations and plugging in numbers to obtain answers. This approach works some of the time, but when problems contain some subtlety, students become stumped and do not know how to get started. One of the primary goals of a physics class is to help students become proficient at solving problems, thus, we as instructors need to help students acquire productive skills and behaviors. Since problem solving permeates all of physics instruction, we have already discussed several problem solving activities in the previous two chapters. In this chapter we focus specifically on problem solving and review student approaches to solving problems and some evidence-based instructional practices (EBIPs) for helping students adopt a more holistic problem solving approach.

4.1.1. Research on problem solving skills and approaches

Early research into problem solving in physics focused on differences between experienced problem solvers or "experts" and inexperienced solvers or "novices." As we reviewed in Chapter 3, experts classify problems according to the concepts and principles used to solve them, whereas novices focus on surface features, like the objects in the problem (springs, pulleys, inclined planes, etc.), or the quantities given in the problem, like velocity and acceleration (Chi et al., 1981; Docktor et al., 2012). This implies that there are major differences in the way the knowledge of problems is organized in memory for experts and novices (Eylon & Reif, 1984; Reif & Heller, 1982; Zajchowski & Martin, 1993). As a problem solver becomes more experienced, knowledge can become "chunked" together with concepts and procedures for solving problems about a particular topic. This reduces cognitive load to free up working memory space (Sweller, 1988).

When faced with a problem, students will use a variety of approaches and strategies. Sometimes these approaches are effective in the short term to get an answer but are ineffective for long term learning and retention. For example, students might immediately look for equations that contain the quantities given in the problem and start plugging in numbers, an approach called "plug and chug," or they might use a similarity-based approach where they find a previously solved problem that looks similar to the new problem and "pattern match" the solution (Gick, 1986; Tuminaro & Redish, 2007; Walsh et al., 2007). They might use "means–ends analysis" to examine what they are given and what they are trying to find and search for ways to reduce the gap between the two (Gick, 1986). A more scientific approach taken by experienced problem solvers involves performing an initial qualitative analysis of the problem based on concepts and principles and then plan out the solution procedure prior to writing down equations (Larkin et al., 1980; Walsh et al., 2007). The planning process might involve breaking up the problem into relevant goals and sub-goals, a process called problem decomposition (Gick, 1986). Expert-like approaches have also been referred to as schema-driven strategies since the initial qualitative representations of the question might cue the application of a particular schema containing concepts and principles along with appropriate procedures for applying those principles (Gick, 1986). A schema in psychology refers to a mental construct that helps the user organize experiences and situations.

Adams and Weiman (2015) identified forty-four subskills involved in problem solving, broken into three different categories. Students need to have specific kinds of *knowledge*, such as basic mathematical knowledge for addition/subtraction/multiplication/division, along with reading comprehension and some real-world knowledge to make sense of situations. They need to be able to engage in several different kinds of *processes*, such as visualizing the problem, planning ways to get an answer, judging the usefulness of information, adaptability and checking calculations. There are also several *beliefs, expectations, and motivation* factors that can influence problem solving ability. For example, students may have an inappropriate attitude that emphasizes memorization over deeply understanding the material, or beliefs about the kind of effort required to make sense of physics (Elby, 2001; Redish *et al.*, 1998).

Others have highlighted the importance of metacognitive skills throughout the problem solving process, where the term *metacognition* refers to thinking about your own thinking. For example, successful solvers periodically monitor their progress toward a solution with questions such as, "Does this process make sense or is the solution getting too messy? Am I still making progress toward the goal of the problem?" They also look back at the end to evaluate their solution for reasonableness, for example, checking the magnitude of the numerical answer, units of the final answer, or using limiting cases in an expression to check for consistency.

When viewing worked example problems, *self-explanations* can be a useful metacognitive tool where students try to make sense of the information by explaining what is going on in the solution to themselves based on what they already know (Chi et al., 1989). This is akin to keeping a mental dialogue while reading, stopping to periodically ask whether what you are reading makes sense or if you have questions about the material. Frequent opportunities to receive feedback on their learning can help students identify their personal strengths and weaknesses and prompt them to reflect on how they will prepare for future assignments and assessments. Mason and Singh (2010) found that giving students opportunities for peer reflections helped students learn more effective problem solving strategies. During the reflections, small groups of students met to discuss homework problem solutions and identify characteristics that made some solutions superior to others. In the next sections, we review additional strategies you can use as an instructor to promote productive problem-solving skills and behaviors in your courses.

4.1.2. Problem representation is important

There are many different ways to write a physics problem, and different formats can significantly impact the solution approaches and strategies used by students. The term *representation* generally refers to the way information is described or depicted, such as with a model or picture. Examples of representations relevant for physics problems include text or verbal representations, diagrammatic, mathematical/symbolic, and graphical (Meltzer, 2005). Although his study focused on multiple choice questions, Meltzer

(2005) observed that students gave inconsistent answers to different representations of the same question. Kohl and Finkelstein (2005) and De Cock (2012) found similar results for homework and quiz problems presented in those four different representations.

Follow-up studies focused on how experts and novices use representations while solving problems. Kohl *et al.* (2007) observed that for challenging problems, students who drew a free-body diagram outperformed students who did not draw a diagram. There was a small subset of students who did not include a diagram yet had a correct solution, so it is possible that they were very comfortable with the material and kept track of information mentally rather than writing it down on paper. When the problem was too easy or straightforward, it was possible for students to plug-and-chug to a correct answer without including a diagram. Kohl and Finkelstein (2008) observed that both experts and novices used similar representations when solving problems with familiar contexts, such as drawing a free-body diagram (likely because students had been instructed in this manner). Where they found differences was in particular stages of the problem solving process, such as analysis and exploration. Experts spent more of their time using representations to identify specific goals or sub-goals for the problem, whereas novices lacked a clear purpose for their representation use.

As you have likely observed in your own courses, students perform significantly worse on questions that are purely symbolic compared to ones where they are given numbers (Torigoe & Gladding, 2011). Other features that can make a problem more difficult include unfamiliar contexts or atypical situations, excess information or missing information, two or more principles required for a solution, a choice of possible principles, abstract principles, mathematical complexity (such as vector components, lengthy algebra, calculus or simultaneous equations), and vague statements such as no explicit target variable (Heller & Hollabaugh, 1992). The question of whether providing a supportive diagram in the problem statement helps or hinders students has resulted in mixed findings. Maries and Singh (2018) found that students performed worse on some problems where they were provided a diagram, particularly for electrostatics contexts. A study with eye-tracking data showed that students spent less time reading the text of a problem when a diagram was included with the problem statement, but providing a diagram did not necessarily lead to a higher proportion of correct responses (Susac et al., 2019).

Since standard problems presented in textbooks are typically well-defined, researchers have developed a host of alternate types of problems to promote conceptual understanding and physics reasoning in more realistic contexts (Hsu et al., 2004). As reviewed in previous chapters, *categorization* tasks can be used to help students practice identifying relevant concepts and principles for a problem without actually going through the process of solving the problem (Dufresne et al., 1992; Hardiman et al., 1989). As described in Chapter 3, students could also be presented with a solution that contains a conceptual error and be asked to identify the error, a task called *finding errors* (Docktor et al., 2015). Additional examples include context-rich problems (Heller & Hollabaugh, 1992), problem posing (Mestre, 2002), jeopardy problems (Van Heuvelen & Maloney, 1999), ranking tasks (O'Kuma et al., 2000), synthesis problems (Ding et al., 2011) and real-world problems. Each of these alternate problem types encourage students to make decisions and explicitly consider the conceptual aspects of physics relevant for problem solving, as we will now describe.

In problem posing, students are presented with a situation (such as a diagram of two blocks connected by a string) along with a concept scenario and they must generate a problem statement that matches both the situation and concepts (Mestre, 2002). This notion of generating a problem statement is similar to jeopardy problems that present students with a part of a problem (such as a diagram or equation) and ask them to devise a situation that could match with the presented information, essentially working backward to write the question (Van Heuvelen & Maloney, 1999).

Ranking tasks are conceptual exercises that provide a list of several variations of a physical situation, oftentimes between four to eight different diagrams or pictures and ask students to rank them according to some criteria (O'Kuma *et al.*, 2000). Synthesis problems combine two physics concepts that are separated in a typical course timeline (Ding *et al.*, 2011). Since most end-of-chapter problems in a textbook typically only address a narrow range of topics and even sometimes label problems with a section header indicating the key topics and equations, this helps draw students' attention away from equations and toward selecting relevant concepts when solving problems. When students struggled to solve synthesis problems, Ding *et al.* (2011) found that providing a series of conceptual questions helped to guide students toward a solution.

Real-world problems use data and measurements from real-life situations to construct physics questions (see the MIT site https://news.mit.edu/2019/making-it-real-mit-engineering-class-0513). The data could include pictures of videos of situations. These problems have some similarities to the instructional approach called Problem-Based Learning or PBL (Duch *et al.*, 2001). In PBL, students work together in collaborative groups to analyze, research, and solve complex real-world problems and communicate their findings. Both of these approaches help to motivate students by illustrating the relevance of physics in everyday life situations.

Below we have provided some examples of different types of physics questions.

Traditional textbook-style problem with numbers
A 200-kg block sits on a ramp that is inclined at $\theta = 37.0$ degrees above the horizontal. The coefficients of static and kinetic friction between the block and the ramp are $\mu_s = 0.60$ and $\mu_k = 0.40$, respectively.

(a) What *horizontal* force F is required to keep the block stationary?
(b) If the horizontal force is removed, what is the block's speed after it slides 3.0 m down the ramp?

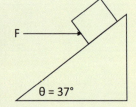

Traditional textbook-style problem without numbers
A block of mass M sits on a ramp that is inclined at θ degrees above the horizontal. The coefficients of static and kinetic friction between the block and the ramp are μ_s and μ_k respectively.

(a) Write an expression for the *horizontal* force F required to keep the block stationary.
(b) If the horizontal force is removed, what is the block's speed after it slides a distance d down the ramp?

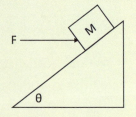

Context Rich Problem
You have a summer job with a professional moving company. You and another mover are unloading a 200-kg wooden crate containing a piano from a truck using a 5-m long steel ramp that is inclined 37 degrees above the horizontal. The cell phone of the other mover rings and they ask you to hold the piano in place during the call. What horizontal force must you apply to keep the piano stationary? You get tired after a few minutes, let go of the piano, and quickly jump out of the way. If the crate is 2 meters wide, what is the piano's speed at the bottom of the ramp? You look in a book giving the properties of materials and find that the coefficient of kinetic friction for wood on steel is 0.40 and the coefficient of static friction is 0.60.

(Continued)

Problem Posing
Pose a problem that could be solved by applying Newton's Second Law by adding a statement or question to the situation below to turn it into a "textbook-like" problem.

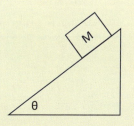

A block of mass M is situated on a inclined plane of angle θ. The coefficients of static and kinetic friction between the block and the ramp are $\mu_s = 0.60$ and $\mu_k = 0.40$, respectively.

Jeopardy Problem
Invent a word problem that is consistent with the following equation:
$(200 \text{ kg})(9.8 \text{ m/s}^2)\sin(37°) - (0.40)(200 \text{ kg})(9.8 \text{ m/s}^2)\cos(37°) = (200 \text{ kg}) a_x$

4.1.3. Problem solving frameworks

One way to think about teaching and learning physics problem solving is a theory called cognitive apprenticeship (Brown *et al.*, 1989; Collins *et al.*, 1987). Like traditional apprenticeship models for learning a trade skill, a novice works closely under the direction of a master to observe and practice the necessary skills of the trade within the situation or context in which it will take place. When this is applied to the classroom, the key pieces of cognitive apprenticeship involve the instructor *modeling* how to perform a skill with explanation while the apprentice (students) attentively observe, then *coaching* the student(s) and offering feedback as they attempt the skills on their own, and providing *scaffolding* to support the specific behavior targeted, and finally fading support structures as the student becomes more proficient at the skill on their own.

When it comes to problem solving instruction, the modeling phase is particularly important—every interaction students have with problem solving sends a message about our expectations. The way you model how to solve example problems during class, the way the textbook structures example problems, and the way homework solutions are written, all influence students' behaviors related to problem solving. If you want to encourage productive behaviors such as "showing your work," you will need to carefully consider the way problem solving is communicated in all aspects of your course. The coaching and scaffolding pieces are also important, such as the grading schemes you use on assessments and the feedback you provide to students on homework, quizzes, or exams. Giving points for things like drawing a diagram or explaining reasoning steps can help to reinforce your expectations for written problem solutions—we know from experience that if you do not grade something, students will not do it since in their minds it does not "count." If you are using online homework systems or computer coaches, you want to ensure that they emphasize the problem solving process and not just the final numerical answer.

Problem solving frameworks or templates can be a useful way to model expectations for students when formatting problem solutions (Hsu *et al.*, 2004). For example, if you want students to start by drawing a picture of the situation and assigning symbols for quantities in the question, you could provide them with a worksheet designating space for that step. If you expect students to solve equations in symbols prior to plugging in numbers, you will need to consistently model that process for them. Several frameworks have been developed for physics instruction to guide students' use of an organized problem solving strategy and break down complex processes used implicitly by experienced solvers (Burkholder *et al.*, 2020; Heller *et al.*, 1992; Heller & Heller, 2000; Van Heuvelen, 1991a, 1991b; Wright & Williams, 1986). As described below, many of these were derived from research in mathematics.

One of the first people to document key steps in the problem solving process was the mathematician Pólya in his book *How to Solve it* (Pólya, 1945). His first step was *Understanding the Problem* including summarizing known and unknown information, introducing suitable notation, and drawing a figure (if relevant to the problem). In step two of *Devising a Plan*, the solver uses their knowledge to plan how to connect the given information to the desired goal in the problem before they engage in *Carrying out the Plan*. The final step is *Looking Back* to examine whether the result makes sense.

Wright and Williams (1986) identified a four-step WISE strategy for solving physics problems to place more emphasis on physics and less emphasis on "number crunching" in their courses:

- **W**hat's happening? (identify physical principles, draw a sketch or diagram, and identify knowns and unknowns)
- **I**solate the unknown (select an equation, solve symbolically, search systematically for other equations as needed)
- **S**ubstitute (plug in numbers and units)
- **E**valuate (check sign, magnitude, and units of the answer)

Although initially they were met with some resistance from students about perceived additional writing, ultimately they found that it improved communication between the instructor and students, increased the accuracy of solutions, and promoted organization of students' solutions. These results are similar to those found with the process of strategy-writing described in Chapter 3 where students first write down the principle they are planning to apply to the problem and a justification for why that principle is applicable, then they write out a procedure for solving the problem (Leonard et al., 1996). The procedure could be formatted as a two-column solution with the plan steps on the left column and the execution of those steps in the right column, also shown in Chapter 3 (Docktor *et al.*, 2015).

Since the first step is critical and fairly involved for solving physics problems, frameworks sometimes subdivide this into more than one step. Heller and Reif (1984) suggested that effective problem solvers first generate a "basic description" that summarizes information about the situation in symbolic, pictorial and verbal forms prior to producing a "theoretical description" that contains diagrams specific to physics concepts and principles. This is reflected in the five-step strategy developed by the Physics Education Research Group at the University of Minnesota (Heller & Heller, 2000; Heller & Hollabaugh, 1992; Heller *et al.*, 1992). This five-step strategy differs from other strategies in that it explicitly asks students to write a solution plan starting from the unknown quantity(ies).

1. **Focus the problem**: draw a picture and write down given information, rephrase question(s) you are trying to answer, general physics approach (key concepts/principles)
2. **Describe the physics**: draw physics-specific diagrams and define quantities, identify target quantity(ies), write quantitative relationships
3. **Plan the solution**: start with an equation which has the target quantity(ies) and identify other unknowns, write additional equations until you have sufficient equations to solve for all the unknowns, then write a plan for solving the equations
4. **Execute the plan**: follow the steps to solve for all unknown quantities you identified in your plan, calculate a numerical value for the target quantity(ies) as applicable, and check units

5. **Evaluate the answer**: check whether the answer is properly stated, unreasonable, and complete

Van Heuvelen (1991b) used a structured problem solving approach as part of the *Overview, Case Study Physics* curriculum to encourage multiple representations of information. Students develop a pictorial representation and identify the given information prior to constructing a physical representation, such as a motion diagram or force diagram. Then they carry out a solution and evaluate the reasonableness of the answer. The framework can be tailored specifically for particular topics such as kinematics or forces.

An example of implementing the Minnesota strategy (Fig. 4.1) and case study physics strategy (Fig. 4.2) are presented in the frameworks below for the context rich piano moving problem presented in the previous section:

> You have a summer job with a professional moving company. You and another mover are unloading a 200-kg wooden crate containing a piano from a truck using a 5-m long steel ramp that is inclined 37 degrees above the horizontal. The cell phone of the other mover rings and they ask you to hold the piano in place during the call. What horizontal force must you apply to keep the piano stationary? You get tired after a few minutes, let go of the piano, and quickly jump out of the way. If the crate is 2 meters wide, what is the piano's speed at the bottom of the ramp? You look in a book giving the properties of materials and find that the coefficient of kinetic friction for wood on steel is 0.40 and the coefficient of static friction is 0.60.

4.1.4. Assessment of problem solving

If you have graded students' problem solutions on quizzes or exams, a standard procedure is to set the total points possible for

FOCUS THE PROBLEM Picture and Given Information

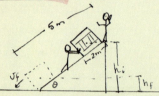

Given: mass of crate $m = 200\,kg$
coefficient of kinetic friction $\mu_k = 0.40$
coefficient of static friction $\mu_s = 0.60$
Ramp is 5m long, crate is 2m wide
$\theta = 37°$

Question(s) What horizontal force is required to keep the crate stationary? What is the crate + piano's speed at the bottom of the ramp?

Approach Use dynamics to find the horizontal force. Find the horizontal and vertical forces acting on the crate. When it is stationary the net force in each direction is zero.
Use conservation of energy to find the speed at the bottom.

DESCRIBE THE PHYSICS
Diagram(s) and Define Quantities

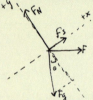

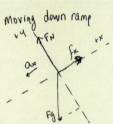

F_N: normal force of incline on ramp
F_g: gravitational force of Earth on crate (called "weight")
F: applied force
f_s: static friction force
f_k: kinetic friction force

Target Quantity(ies) F and v_f

Quantitative Relationships

Components of F

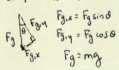

$F_x = F\cos\theta$
$F_y = F\sin\theta$

Components of F_g

$F_{g,x} = F_g \sin\theta$
$F_{g,y} = F_g \cos\theta$
$F_g = mg$

Stationary
$\Sigma F_x = ma_x^0$
$F_x + f_s - F_{g,x} = 0$
$F\cos\theta + \mu_s F_N - mg\sin\theta = 0$

$\Sigma F_y = ma_y^0$
$F_N - F_y - F_{g,y} = 0$
$F_N - F\sin\theta - mg\cos\theta = 0$

moving
$\Sigma F_x = ma_x$
$f_k - F_{g,x} = -ma_x$
$\mu_k F_N - F_g\sin\theta = -ma_x$

$\Sigma F_y = ma_y^0$
$F_N - F_{g,y} = 0$
$F_N - mg\cos\theta = 0$

$K_1 + U_1 + W_{other} = K_2 + U_2$
$0 + mgh + W_{fric} = \tfrac{1}{2}mv^2 + 0$

(Continued)

From Manipulating Equations to a More Conceptual Approach 97

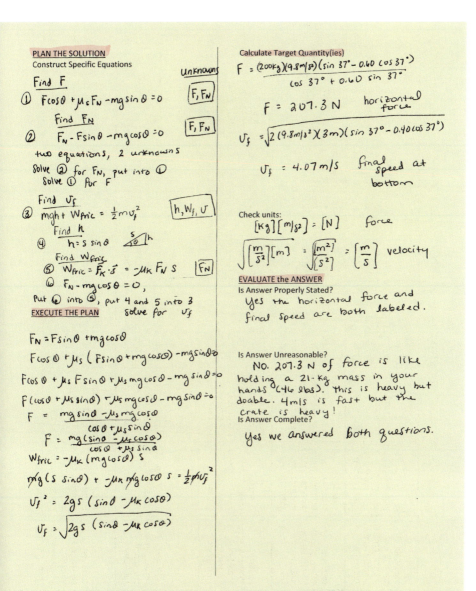

Fig. 4.1. Minnesota five-step problem solving strategy.

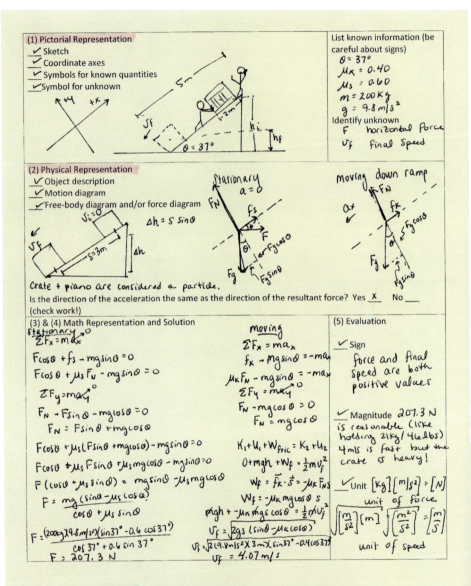

Fig. 4.2. Van Heuvelen strategy from case study physics.

the problem and then assign points to particular components of the solution (or deduct points for particular errors). This allows the instructor some flexibility in weighing problem features and tailoring a grading scheme to different topics or assessment situations. One thing to be cautious of when grading is to stay true to your goals as an instructor. Even if you want students to show their reasoning, research has indicated that instructors are hesitant to deduct points from a sparse solution that might be correct, and they tend to make assumptions about students' thought processes when there are gaps in written work (Henderson et al., 2004). If you are using a particular framework or template, points should be awarded for each aspect of the framework to reinforce the importance to including each step. Some samples of templates and point designations are provided in (Burkholder et al., 2020).

Although there currently are no multiple choice diagnostic assessments for problem solving like there are for concepts, some researchers have focused on developing rubrics for assessing problem solving skills. Docktor et al. (2016) describe the development and validation of the Minnesota Assessment of Problem Solving (MAPS) rubric designed to apply to any problem type or topic. The rubric defines criteria to attain a score in five different areas: organizing problem information into a Useful Description, selecting appropriate concepts and principles in the Physics Approach, the Specific Application of Physics principles to the conditions in the problem, using appropriate Mathematical Procedures, and following an organized procedure or Logical Progression. Each of these criteria are scored on a scale from 0 to 5 or designated as not applicable to the problem or solver. Using a rubric like this can help instructors identify students' strengths and weaknesses related to problem solving skills and target instruction accordingly. The rubric was built on previous rubrics such as the one used in (Heller *et al.*, 1992) for use with context rich problems and cooperative group problem solving. Hull *et al.* (2013) criticize that most problem solving rubrics do not go far enough in valuing the conceptual aspects involved in mathematical procedures, and should be revised to better assess the blending of conceptual and formal mathematical reasoning during those procedures. A copy of the MAPS rubric is provided in Fig. 4.3.

4.2. What are the implications of research on problem solving for instruction?

We offer the following implications of the research reviewed above for instruction:

- **Problem solving needs to be taught explicitly.** Students use a variety of strategies to solve physics problems, and while some of these are effective in the short term they are ineffective for long-term retention and transfer. Instructors need to explicitly model a process for students that emphasizes principles and concepts over equation manipulation, highlighting all of the decisions that have become automatic for solving routine physics exercises.
- **If you do not assess it, students will not do it.** If you expect students to produce carefully written problem solutions and explain their reasoning steps, you will need to design assessment structures in your course to reward those behaviors. It is very easy for instructors to assume that a student with a sparse solution who obtained the correct result "knew what they were doing" and should receive full credit, compared to a student who showed more steps but made a conceptual error along the way

	5	4	3	2	1	0	NA(Problem)	NA(Solver)
USEFUL DESCRIPTION	The description is useful, appropriate, and complete.	The description is useful but contains minor omissions or errors.	Parts of the description are not useful, missing, and/or contain errors.	Most of the description is not useful, missing, and/or contains errors.	The entire description is not useful and/or contains errors.	The solution does not include a description and it is necessary for this problem/solver.	A description is not necessary for this **problem**. (i.e., it is given in the problem statement)	A description is not necessary for this **solver**.
PHYSICS APPROACH	The physics approach is appropriate and complete.	The physics approach contains minor omissions or errors.	Some concepts and principles of the physics approach are missing and/or inappropriate.	Most of the physics approach is missing and/or inappropriate.	All of the chosen concepts and principles are inappropriate.	The solution does not indicate an approach, and it is necessary for this problem/solver.	An explicit physics approach is not necessary for this **problem**. (i.e., it is given in the problem)	An explicit physics approach is not necessary for this **solver**.
SPECIFIC APPLICATION OF PHYSICS	The specific application of physics is appropriate and complete.	The specific application of physics contains minor omissions or errors.	Parts of the specific application of physics are missing and/or contain errors.	Most of the specific application of physics is missing and/or contains errors.	The entire specific application is inappropriate and/or contains errors.	The solution does not indicate an application of physics and it is necessary.	Specific application of physics is not necessary for this **problem**.	Specific application of physics is not necessary for this **solver**.
MATHEMATICAL PROCEDURES	The mathematical procedures are appropriate and complete.	Appropriate mathematical procedures are used with minor omissions or errors.	Parts of the mathematical procedures are missing and/or contain errors.	Most of the mathematical procedures are missing and/or contain errors.	All mathematical procedures are inappropriate and/or contain errors.	There is no evidence of mathematical procedures, and they are necessary.	Mathematical procedures are not necessary for this **problem** or are very simple.	Mathematical procedures are not necessary for this **solver**.
LOGICAL PROGRESSION	The entire problem solution is clear, focused, and logically connected.	The solution is clear and focused with minor inconsistencies	Parts of the solution are unclear, unfocused, and/or inconsistent.	Most of the solution parts are unclear, unfocused, and/or inconsistent.	The entire solution is unclear, unfocused, and/or inconsistent.	There is no evidence of logical progression, and it is necessary.	Logical progression is not necessary for this **problem**. (i.e, one-step)	Logical progression is not necessary for this **solver**.

Fig. 4.3. Minnesota Assessment of Problem Solving (MAPS) rubric.

(Henderson *et al.*, 2004). It has been shown that students can solve a complex physics problem flawlessly but have a flawed conceptual understanding of it (Morphew & Mestre, 2018). It is important to use consistent scoring criteria and check assumptions.
- **Students have attitudes, beliefs and expectations that impact performance in physics.** Problem solving in physics is a complex process that can require students to stay motivated and persistent. Sometimes beliefs about learning physics can impact performance, like a belief that physics is a set of disconnected facts and equations to be memorized rather than a network of connected concepts. Students might have attitudes toward learning physics that favor getting an answer rather than understanding the appropriate procedures and methods for reaching that answer. Instructors should be cognizant of students' expectations and how they can impact learning.

4.3. Examples of teaching interventions based on learning research

The research reviewed in this chapter, as well as our teaching experiences, indicate that the following strategies can be useful for promoting skilled problem solving in your courses.
- **Implement a problem solving framework to guide students' problem solutions.** Providing a framework or template for students can help students who just "don't know where to start" and can promote a more organized solution process. Most of these frameworks begin with drawing a sketch or picture of the situation and clearly assigning symbols for quantities. Some frameworks have students explicitly plan out their solutions before

carrying out the equation manipulation and mathematical calculations. In this chapter, we reviewed at least four different strategies and frameworks you could use. Actually providing students with a worksheet template can help to scaffold this process for them until they naturally follow the procedure on their own.
- **Carefully select problems for your course(s).** There are many different formats and styles for writing physics problems. You will want to choose problems that discourage common student behaviors like equation hunting and chug-and-plug problem solving. So-called "traditional" end-of-chapter problems include artificial situations like blocks and pulleys on inclined planes and may have multiple parts but this is not necessarily optimal for your particular students. In writing problems you will have to decide things like whether to include a diagram or not, numbers or no numbers, symbols for quantities provided in the question or not, and the difficulty of the mathematics required. There are several research-based ways to write alternate formats for problems which were reviewed in this chapter, including context-rich problems, problem posing, jeopardy problems, ranking task exercises, synthesis problems and real-world problems.
- **Model and assess productive problem solving behaviors.** When implementing an EBIP, such as a problem solving framework, it is also important to model procedures for students when solving example problems on the board or in virtual worked examples. Explicitly verbalize the decisions you are making and the conditions under which a particular physics principle is applicable. Help students connect math skills with physics reasoning and minimize the use of nonfundamental formulae to discourage the

memorization of situation-specific equations (Zajchowski & Martin, 1993). You will also need to model appropriate behaviors in written solutions to homework, quizzes, or exams as applicable. Solutions provided by textbook companies as instructor solution manuals are typically very sparse and missing steps—they are better suited for instructors to view, not students.

Along with modeling productive problem solving behaviors, it is also important to reinforce those behaviors in the way you assess students' solutions. Assign points to each step of the process or of the written template so students are rewarded for the process and not just the final result. You could also implement research-based instructional tools such as intelligent tutors, computer coaches, or online homework systems to help students practice problem solving skills—providing those systems are aligned with the practices you are trying to encourage in your course.

- **Encourage the development of metacognitive skills for problem solving.** We want students to be reflective about their learning when solving problems and how they might apply what they have learned to future problems. When students view worked example problems, encourage them to use *self-explanations* to make sense of the procedures. After they solve a problem, encourage students to evaluate the reasonableness of their answer. Provide students with frequent opportunities to receive feedback on their performance and reflect on their learning.

References

Adams, W.K. & Wieman, C.E. (2015). Analyzing the many skills involved in solving complex physics problems. *American Journal of Physics*, **83**(5), 459–467. http://dx.doi.org/10.1119/1.4913923

Brown, J.S., Collins, A. & Duguid, P. (1989). Situated cognition and the culture of learning. *Educational researcher*, **18**(1), 32–42.

Burkholder, E.W., Miles, J.K., Layden, T.J., Wang, K.D., Fritz, A.V. & Wieman, C.E. (2020). Template for teaching and assessment of problem solving in introductory physics. *Physical Review Physics Education Research*, **16**(010123), 1–20. https://doi.org/10.1103/PhysRevPhysEducRes.16.010123

Collins, A., Brown, J.S. & Newman, S.E. (1987). Cognitive apprenticeship: Teaching the craft of reading, writing and mathematics (Technical Report no. 403). BBN Laboratories, Cambridge, MA. Centre for the Study of Reading, University of Illinois, January, 1987.

Chi, M.T.H., Bassok, M., Lewis, M.W., Reimann, P. & Glaser, R. (1989). Self-explanations: How students study and use examples in learning to solve problems. *Cognitive Science*, **13**(2), 145–182.

Chi, M.T.H., Feltovich, P.J. & Glaser, R. (1981). Categorization and representation of physics problems by experts and novices. *Cognitive Science*, **5**, 121–152.

De Cock, M. (2012). Representation use and strategy choice in physics problem solving. *Physical Review Special Topics – Physics Education Research*, **8**(020117), 1–15. http://dx.doi.org/10.1103/PhysRevSTPER.8.020117

Ding, L., Reay, N., Lee, A. & Bao, L. (2011). Exploring the role of conceptual scaffolding in solving synthesis problems. *Physical Review Special Topics – Physics Education Research*, **7**(020109).

Docktor, J.L., Dornfeld, J., Frodermann, E., Heller, K., Hsu, L., Jackson, K.A., Mason, A., Ryan, Q.X. & Yang, J. (2016). Assessing student written problem solutions: A problem solving rubric with application to introductory physics. *Physical Review – Physics Education Research*, **12**(010130), 1–18. http://dx.doi.org/10.1103/PhysRevPhysEducRes.12.010130

Docktor, J.L, Mestre, J.P. & Ross, B.H. (2012). Impact of a short intervention on novices' categorization criteria. *Physical Review-Special Topics: Physics Education Research*, **8**(020102), 1–11. https://doi.org/10.1103/PhysRevSTPER.8.020102

Docktor, J.L., Strand, N.E., Mestre, J.P. & Ross, B.H. (2015). Conceptual problem solving in high school physics. *Physical Review Special Topics – Physics Education Research*, **11**(020106), 1–13. https://doi.org/10.1103/PhysRevSTPER.11.020106

Duch, B.J., Groh, S.E. & Allen, D.E. (2001). *The Power of Problem-based Learning* (1st Ed.) Sterling, Virginia: Stylus Publishing, LLC.

Dufresne, R., Gerace, W.J., Hardiman, P.T. & Mestre, J.P. (1992). Constraining novices to perform expert-like problem analyses: Effects on schema acquisition. *Journal of the Learning Sciences*, **2**, 307–331. https://doi.org/10.1207/s15327809jls0203_3

Elby, A. (2001). Helping physics students learn how to learn. *American Journal of Physics*, **69**(7), S54–S64. https://doi.org/10.1119/1.1377283

Eylon, B. & Reif, F. (1984). Effects of knowledge organization on task performance. *Cognition and Instruction*, **1**(1), 5–44. https://www.jstor.org/stable/3233519

Gick, M.L. (1986). Problem-solving strategies. *Educational Psychologist*, **21**(1&2), 99–120. https://doi.org/10.1080/00461520.1986.9653026

Hardiman, P.T., Dufresne, R. & Mestre, J.P. (1989). The relation between problem categorization and problem solving among novices and experts. *Memory & Cognition*, **17**, 627–638.

Heller, J.I. & Reif, F. (1984). Prescribing effective human problem-solving processes: Problem description in physics. *Cognition and Instruction*, **1**(2), 177–216. https://doi.org/10.1207/s1532690xci0102_2

Heller, K. & Heller, P. (2000). *Competent Problem Solver – Calculus Version*. New York: McGraw-Hill.

Heller, P. & Hollabaugh, M. (1992). Teaching problem solving through cooperative grouping. Part 2: Designing problems and structuring groups. *American Journal of Physics*, **60**(7), 637–644. https://doi.org/10.1119/1.17118

Heller, P., Keith, R. & Anderson, S. (1992). Teaching problem solving through cooperative grouping. Part 1: Group versus individual problem solving. *American Journal of Physics*, **60**(7), 627–636. http://dx.doi.org/10.1119/1.17117

Henderson, C., Yerushalmi, E., Kuo, V., Heller, P. & Heller, K. (2004). Grading student problem solutions: The challenge of sending a consistent message. *American Journal of Physics*, **72**(2), 164–169. https://doi.org/10.1119/1.1634963

Hull, M.M., Kuo, E., Gupta, A. & Elby, A. (2013). Problem solving rubrics revisited: Attending to blending of informal conceptual and formal mathematical reasoning. *Physical Review Special Topics – Physics Education Research*, **9**(010105).

Hsu, L., Brewe, E., Foster, T.M. & Harper, K.A. (2004). Resource letter RPS-1: Research in problem solving. *American Journal of Physics*, **72**(9), 1147–1156. https://doi.org/10.1119/1.1763175

Kohl, P.B. & Finkelstein, N.D. (2005). Student representational competence and self-assessment when solving physics problems. *Physical Review Special Topics – Physics Education Research*, **1**(010104).

Kohl, P.B. & Finkelstein, N.D. (2008). Patterns of multiple representation use by experts and novices during physics problem solving. *Physical Review Special Topics – Physics Education Research*, **4**(010111), 1–10.

Kohl, P.B. Rosengrant, D. & Finkelstein, N.D. (2007). Strongly and weakly directed approaches to teaching multiple representation use in physics. *Physical Review Special Topics – Physics Education Research*, **3**(010108).

Larkin, J.H., McDermott, J., Simon, D.P. & Simon, H.A. (1980). Models of competence in solving physics problems. *Cognitive Science*, **4**, 317–345.

Leonard, W.J., Dufresne, R.J. & Mestre, J.P. (1996). Using qualitative problem-solving strategies to highlight the role of conceptual knowledge in solving problems. *American Journal of Physics*, **64**(12), 1495–1503.

Maries, A. & Singh, S. (2018). Case of two electrostatics problems: Can providing a diagram adversely impact physics tsudents' problem solving performance? *Physical Review Physics Education Research*, **14**(010114).

Mason, A. & Singh, C. (2010. Helping students learn effective problem solving strategies by reflecting with peers. *American Journal of Physics*, **78**(7), 748–754.

Meltzer, D.E. (2005). Relation between students' problem-solving performance and representational format. *American Journal of Physics*, **73**(5), 463–478.

Mestre, J.P. (2002). Probing adults' conceptual understanding and transfer of learning via problem posing. *Journal of Applied Developmental Psychology*, **23**(1), 9–50. https://doi.org/10.1016/S0193-3973(01)00101-0

Morphew, J.W. & Mestre, J.P. (2018). Exploring the connection between problem solving and conceptual understanding in physics. *Revista de Enseñanza de la Física*, **30**(2), 75–85.

O'Kuma, T.L., Maloney, S.P. & Hieggelke, C.J. (2000). *Ranking Task Exercises in Physics* (Prentice-Hall, Upper Saddle River, NJ).

Polya, G. (1945). *How to Solve it*. Princeton, NJ: Princeton University Press.

Redish, E.F., Saul, J.M. & Steinberg, R.N. (1998). Student expectations in introductory physics. *American Journal of Physics*, **66**(3), 212–224. https://doi.org/10.1119/1.18847

Reif, F. & Heller, J.I. (1982). Knowledge structure and problem solving in physics. *Educational Psychologist*, **17**(2), 102–127. https://doi.org/10.1080/00461528209529248

Susac, A., Bubic, A., PLaninic, M., Movre, M. & Palmovic, M. (2019). Role of diagrams in problem solving: An evaluation of eye-tracking parameters as a measure of visual attention. *Physical Review Special Topics – Physics Education Research*, **15**(013101).

Sweller, J. (1988). Cognitive load during problem solving: Effects on learning. *Cognitive Science*, **12**, 257–285. https://doi.org/10.1207/s15516709cog1202_4

Torigoe, E.T. & Gladding, G.E. (2011). Connecting symbolic difficulties with failure in physics. *American Journal of Physics*, **79**(1), 133–140.

Tuminaro, J. & Redish, E.F. (2007). Elements of a cognitive model of physics problem solving: Epistemic games. *Physical Review Special Topics – Physics Education Research*, **3**(020101), 1–22. https://doi.org/10.1103/PhysRevSTPER.3.020101

Van Heuvelen, A. (1991a). Learning to think like a physicist: A review of research-based instructional strategies. *American Journal of Physics*, **59**(10), 891–897.

Van Heuvelen, A. (1991b). Overview, case study physics. *American Journal of Physics*, **59**(10), 898–907. https://doi.org/10.1119/1.16668

Van Heuvelen, A. & Maloney. D. (1999). Playing physics jeopardy. *American Journal of Physics*, **67**(3), 252–256. https://doi.org/10.1119/1.19233

Walsh, L.N., Howard, R.G. & Bowe, B. (2007). Phenomenographic study of students' problem solving approaches in physics. *Physical Review Special Topics – Physics Education Research*, **3**(020108), 1–12. https://doi.org/10.1103/PhysRevSTPER.3.020108

Wright, D.S. & Williams, C.D. (1986). A WISE strategy for introductory physics. *The Physics Teacher*, **24**, 211–216. https://doi.org/10.1119/1.2341986

Zajchowski, R. & Martin, J. (1993). Differences in the problem solving of stronger and weaker novices in physics: Knowledge, strategies, or knowledge structure? *Journal of Research in Science Teaching*, **30**(5), 459–470. https://doi.org/10.1002/tea.3660300505

Chapter

5 Active Learning Strategies:
Engaging Students in their Own Learning is the Key to Learning

5.1. What does the research tell us?

If you teach physics or another area of STEM, there is a good chance that you have heard some buzz about "active learning" instructional strategies. Maybe you have even tried some innovative teaching methods in your classes with varied degrees of success. Despite a growing body of literature in support of active learning, the phenomenon has not spread as widely as might be expected (Freeman *et al.*, 2014; Henderson & Dancy, 2007, 2009). In this chapter, we explore not only what active learning looks like in a physics classroom but also examine the challenges associated with implementation.

5.1.1. Introduction and background

Active instructional approaches have their roots in constructivist learning theory, as discussed in Chapter 2—when we encounter new information, we try to make sense of it based on our existing ideas and experiences (NRC, 2000). Learning is an active process of constructing knowledge, either cognitively engaging with material or being physically active or both. As a result, the extent to which students can effectively construct new knowledge depends on the nature of their prior knowledge;

prior knowledge could be accurate but insufficient, or could be inappropriate (sometimes called misconceptions or alternative conceptions). For example, recall from Chapters 1 and 2 that students might have an erroneous idea that heavier objects fall faster than lighter ones or that in a collision between two objects the bigger one exerts a larger force on the smaller one. The "teaching by telling" lecture-based instructional approach has been shown to be ineffective for addressing misconceptions and facilitating long-term knowledge construction. This does not mean you should never lecture—it just should not be the only tool in your toolbox. There may be some situations for which lecturing is the most efficient way to convey information, however being an effective educator typically means blending a variety of strategies and methods to fit your context (NRC, 2000, 2012b, 2013; Schwartz & Bransford, 1998).

Constructivist epistemology also emphasizes the importance of learners discovering or figuring things out for themselves (Bruner, 1961). This does not mean students should simply be left to their own devices to flounder with material; the instructor still plays an important role in structuring learning activities and serving as a facilitator or coach to guide students toward appropriate scientific thinking. This is consistent with the idea that learning and cognition are sociocultural by nature; students can make meaning from their observations, and interactions with others (Bandura, 1986; Vygotsky, 1978).

As we examine active learning strategies in this chapter, it will become evident that several of them incorporate metacognition and overlap with formative assessment techniques. Metacognition is the notion of getting students thinking about their own thinking, such as reflecting on their reasoning processes or what they have learned. This can be as straightforward as a student periodically questioning themselves: *Does this information make sense to me? How does this relate to what I already know? What questions do I have about this material?* or it could be more explicitly structured into course activities, such as an instructor prompting students to reflect: *What were the key physics principles and procedures we used to solve this problem?* Metacognitive strategies that help students monitor their own learning have been shown to boost learning and transfer (NRC, 2000). In order to teach with metacognition in mind, instructors might implement classroom strategies to make students' thinking visible to themselves and the instructor. These strategies are oftentimes referred to as formative assessment classroom techniques (FACTs) (Keeley, 2008). The term *formative* broadly means that assessment is happening during the process of instruction to help instructors identify students' strengths and weaknesses and inform the next steps for the teaching and learning process. It is assessment *for* learning, not just assessment of learning (Chappuis, 2015).

What exactly is "active learning" and what does it look like in a physics classroom? The "traditional" lecture-based physics class is usually described in the following way: the instructor does most of the talking while deriving physics definitions and theories, perhaps also illustrating how to solve quantitative problems. Students passively copy down notes, and are expected to apply the information to algorithmic problem solving exercises that appear at the end of the textbook chapter (Dancy & Henderson, 2007; Docktor & Mestre, 2014; Hake, 1998). Students might also attend laboratory sessions where they follow step by step instructions to confirm or verify their experimental consistency with physics principles. Almost anything that deviates from this "traditional" view of instruction is colloquially referred to as active learning or interactive engagement (IE) techniques (Hake, 1998).

The entire field of Physics Education Research arose due to a general dissatisfaction with student learning in traditional physics classrooms, when instructors observed how students could get a correct numerical answer to a problem, but they could not explain the concepts (Cummings, 2011; Meltzer & Otero, 2015; Morphew & Mestre, 2018), or displayed conceptual understanding that did not conform with physics principles (i.e., misconceptions). Some researchers suggest that in order to earn the label of an "active learning" strategy, the instructional approach needs to be grounded in research on student learning (Meltzer & Thornton, 2012). Therefore, these practices are also referred to as evidence-based instructional practices (EBIPs) or research-based instructional strategies (RBIS) (Dancy & Henderson, 2007). Non-traditional or alternative instruction includes significant student–student discourse focusing on students' ideas, and students being physically active (interacting with equipment and materials). Other disciplines might refer to these as *student-centered* instructional approaches because students are afforded more control over their learning (NRC, 2012b). A summary of key elements is provided below, see (Meltzer & Thornton, 2012; Mestre 2001).

Characteristics of active-learning instruction could include:

- Providing opportunities for students to share their ideas and reasoning, either individually or with small groups of peers
- Encouraging qualitative reasoning based on physics concepts (which is discussed in Chapter 2)
- Encouraging construction and sense-making of physics knowledge; for example, students are prompted to figure things out for themselves

- Providing opportunities for students to engage in the process of "doing science"
- Providing opportunities for students to apply their knowledge flexibly across multiple contexts (that is, to practice "transferring" their knowledge to novel contexts)
- Incorporating formative assessment techniques to monitor student learning and inform instruction
- Helping students organize content knowledge according to some hierarchy (which is discussed in Chapter 3)
- Teaching metacognitive strategies to students; for example, students reflect on their own reasoning and problem solving practices

Teaching using active learning strategies means changing common classroom "norms" to a culture where students are willing to share their ideas even if those ideas end up being incorrect (NRC, 2000). Students need to be willing to work together as a team, take risks, and revise their thinking when new information arises. Promoting these community-based attitudes toward learning can prove challenging, especially for students who have extensive experience in more individualistic, competitive learning environments.

At the university level, physics courses can take a variety of formats. Some institutions have "lecture" that is taught separately from a laboratory portion of a course, whereas other institutions combine these two into an integrated lab-lecture format called a studio format (Wilson, 1994), or *Workshop Physics* (Laws, 2004). Some institutions have a weekly recitation or discussion session that is separate from lecture and lab whereas others do not. Learning can also take place outside of formal classroom environments as students complete homework, meet with study groups or tutors, interact with online course management systems or technology-enhanced resources (computer simulations, etc.) As a result, research-based instructional strategies and research-based curricula developed in physics tend to target a particular classroom environment. Some of the most prevalent RBIS are highlighted in the sections below, however a more comprehensive list of strategies and assessment tools is provided in the resource PhysPort, https://www.physport.org/

5.1.2. Reforming the "traditional" lecture classroom

For instructors looking to "get their feet wet" with active learning, most choose to make small changes to traditional lectures to provide opportunities for students to pause and reflect on their learning during class and/or share their reasoning by discussing physics concepts with peers during class (Henderson & Dancy, 2009). One example is the formative assessment technique called think-pair-share (Keeley, 2008; Lyman, 1981). Students are presented a question by the instructor and are given time to think about it on their own first, then they pair up with another student to discuss their thinking (see sample problems at the end of Chapter 3 for questions that work well in this context). Some pairs might be selected to share their ideas with the class as a whole. This general strategy was more formally introduced to the physics community in Eric Mazur's 1997 book on *Peer Instruction*, although it was already in use without that label, see (Dufresne et al., 1996). In early versions of *Peer Instruction*, students complete a pre-class reading and answer questions about the reading using a method similar to *Just in Time Teaching* (Novak et al., 1999). The instructor uses those responses to design challenging multiple choice questions called *ConcepTests* to present during the whole-class lecture period. These questions typically focus on physics concepts and some of the options may include "distractor" choices based on common student difficulties. The class goes something like this: After 7–10 minutes of lecture, the instructor stops and presents a conceptual question. Students first reflect on the question and commit to an individual answer (either electronically or using flash cards) and the instructor reviews and/or displays the response distribution. Then students are given 1–2 minutes to discuss their ideas with peer(s) and revote on an answer choice. Based on the responses, the instructor decides whether more explanation is needed or whether to move on to the next concept. This process typically takes 5–8 minutes, so by repeating the steps a one-hour lecture is broken into approximately four 15-minute chunks of time. To optimize interactions, Mazur suggests that the initial proportion of students answering correctly should be between 35% and 70% (Crouch & Mazur, 2001; Redish, 2003), however other studies have shown that peer discussion enhances understanding even when no one in the peer group knows the correct answer (Smith et al., 2009); nothing is better at getting students' attention than when the entire class misses a seemingly easy conceptual question, thereby creating an opportunity for learning. Conceptual understanding is also reinforced in other aspects of the course by including conceptual multiple choice questions on exams.

One advantage of the *Peer Instruction* method is that the instructor can see an "anonymous" (or not so anonymous) view of what the whole class thinks, rather than getting a limited view of students' understanding based on verbal replies to a question from a few students. The class can then be better tailored to students' needs. An advantage for students is that they are more engaged during class and get immediate feedback on their level of understanding of course material. There is also support for the method from hundreds of research publications from a variety of STEM disciplines. Most of these show higher gains on diagnostic concept inventories (Crouch & Mazur, 2001; Freeman et al., 2014) or positive effects on students' attitudes toward learning physics (Zhang et al., 2017), however the effects on quantitative problem solving are less clear (McDaniel et al., 2016). Some challenges with the method include time management decisions on the part of the instructor. With less time spent on traditional lecture, the instructor has to decide whether to only discuss a portion of material in class and expect students to learn the rest on their own through readings, recitation sessions, and homework; or to decrease the number of topics covered in a course (Crouch & Mazur, 2001). One approach developed at the University of Illinois and now commercially available and used in many universities across the country (see www.flipitphysics.com) "outsources" presentation of basic information/concepts to 15-minute web-based, interactive "pre-lectures" that students view prior to coming to class, which allows the instructor to refine understanding rather than present new material; this method does not reduce the amount of material covered in a typical introductory course. *Peer Instruction* places higher emphasis on concepts rather than quantitative problem solving, so students must learn those skills during other aspects of the course (such as in recitation sections). In addition, students vary in their reactions to active learning methods and some may be resistant to non-traditional methods (we discuss barriers to reformed instruction at the end of this chapter).

Another example of a lecture-based instructional strategy with similar features is *Interactive Lecture Demonstrations* or ILDs (Sokoloff & Thornton, 1997, 2004). Instead of presenting students with a conceptual based multiple choice question, students are shown the equipment for a demonstration and asked to make a prediction (such as predicting the shape of a force vs time graph). After making an individual prediction, students engage in a discussion with neighboring students and the instructor elicits responses from the class. Students record their final predictions and the instructor carries out the demonstration with measurements. Then the instructor facilitates a class discussion about the results, and how to extend those results to different physical situations based on the same concepts. This method also shares similarities with the formative assessment technique called P-O-E for predict, observe, and explain (Keeley, 2008). Similar to other RBIS, *Interactive Lecture Demonstrations* have shown higher gains on concept inventories than traditional instruction (Sokoloff & Thornton, 1997, 2004). Another study found that having students predict and discuss demonstrations had a greater effect on performance on a free response test compared to students who just observed the demonstration and heard the teacher's explanation (Crouch *et al.*, 2004).

Other general strategies exist for making lectures more interactive, referred to as formative assessment classroom techniques or FACTs (Keeley, 2008). One of the most common examples is the *think-pair-share* strategy discussed above. Additional examples include: Pausing during class for students to reflect on their learning and write something down (such as a muddiest point, point of most significance in the lesson, or general minute paper), creating concept maps, KWL chart (students write down what they **K**now, **W**ant to know, and what they've **L**earned), or incorporating mini whiteboards as collaboration tools for students. Students could also collaborate on solving physics problems during lecture (this is discussed further in the next section with regard to recitation and discussion sessions).

5.1.3. Reforming the traditional laboratory or recitation experience

Even though laboratories are somewhat *active* in that students interact with equipment and each other, traditional laboratory classes are referred to as "cookbook-style" because they provide step-by-step instructions for students to follow. Efforts to reform the physics laboratory experience to be more engaging typically focus on the lab activities and curricula themselves, reforming instructions to incorporate more decision making on the part of students and encouraging them to figure things out with less guidance. One challenge with implementing new laboratory activities is that additional training might be required for faculty to learn about the RBIS or the technology associated with the curriculum. Although computer-based tools for data collection and analysis have become quite common in physics classrooms, it is possible that a particular institution might have to make a financial investment to maintain equipment and software licenses. For institutions with undergraduate and/or graduate teaching assistants, training might also be necessary for them to carry out instruction as intended by curriculum developers. Some example laboratory curricula are highlighted below.

The *Investigative Science Learning Environment (ISLE)* encourages students to engage in a cycle of learning that is modeled after the way physicists create knowledge (Etkina & Van Heuvelen, 2001, 2006). Students encounter an interesting physical phenomenon, gather data and propose multiple explanations, then experimentally test those explanations. Finally, they apply their ideas to real-world problems. ISLE is somewhat unique in its explicit focus on fostering the development of scientific reasoning abilities. The learning system has been adapted into multiple textbooks (see Van Heuvelen & Etkina, 2006) and a set of video-based experiments further described at http://islephysics.net/pt3

The *RealTime Physics (RTP)* laboratories include a mixture of conceptual activities and laboratory experiments (Sokoloff *et al.*, 2004). Investigations typically incorporate technology tools for data collection and analysis, such as sensors that dynamically display graphs of data in "real time." The research-based activities are designed to address common preconceptions students might have about physical situations, encourage students to construct their own models of phenomena, and encourage group work and discussion. Each laboratory includes a set of pre-lab questions and a post-lab assignment to reinforce concepts and skills. *Workshop Physics* is an activity-based curriculum designed for introductory calculus-based physics courses (Laws, 2004), although it shares some of these same characteristics with RTP labs. Students make predictions, conduct qualitative observations and quantitative experiments, construct explanations, and use computer-based tools to collect and analyze data and/or develop mathematical models of phenomena. The use of video-based methods for data collection and analysis are also becoming increasingly common in laboratory curricula, as are interactive simulations such as *Physlets* (Christian & Belloni, 2003) or PhET (https://phet.colorado.edu/).

For physics courses that include a recitation or discussion session, the emphasis is typically on problem solving or an extension of the lecture but with a smaller group of students. One traditional view of the recitation was that it provided opportunities for students to ask questions about homework, or for the TA/instructor to solve additional example problems for students. Efforts to make recitation more "active" typically incorporate small groups and alternative types of problems and/or conceptual worksheets. A discussion-based strategy developed at the University of Minnesota is *Cooperative Group Problem Solving* in conjunction with the use of context-rich problems (Heller et al., 1992; Heller & Hollabaugh, 1992) where it was reported that the quality of problem solutions produced by cooperative groups of students was significantly better than the quality of solutions from individuals in the group on matched problems (even the strongest student in the group). Problem solving instructional methods are reviewed in more detail in Chapter 4.

Another well-known strategy for recitation sessions is referred to generally as tutorials, which are described by the developers as guided-inquiry worksheets where students confront and resolve conceptual difficulties (McDermott & Schaffer, 2002). Questions in a tutorial workbook guide students to reason about concepts and apply their knowledge to real-world situations. They also obtain practice moving flexibly between multiple representations of information (equations, graphs, diagrams, verbal descriptions, etc.) Students complete pre-tests, homework assignments, and post-tests in addition to the worksheets. Several adaptations of tutorial curricula have been created, see PhysPort (https://www.physport.org/Assessment.cfm) for a comprehensive list.

There have been several efforts in the field of physics to redesign classroom spaces and courses to combine lectures and laboratory experiences. Class periods tend to be longer (2 to 2.5 hours) and the classrooms are designed to promote cooperative group work while students work on a variety of tasks, such as hands-on activities, laboratories, conceptual questions, simulations, or problem solving. An early implementation of this is referred to as a *Studio* classroom (Wilson, 1994). The *Workshop Physics* curriculum has been designed for the integrated lab-lecture classroom, however the authors claim it can also be adapted to other settings

(Laws, 2004). *SCALE-UP* (Student-Centered Active Learning for Undergraduate Programs) is a similarly integrated learning environment which incorporates a variety of PER-based learning activities but for a larger class of students (Beichner, 2008; Gaffney *et al.*, 2008). A key challenge with integrated classrooms is that it could require substantial restructuring of the physical space and time blocks of physics courses, which presents a financial and/or logistical challenge. This is cited as a common barrier to reformed instruction, as discussed below.

5.1.4. Reforming the "out-of-class" experience

Not all learning takes place during structured class time, and most courses include an expectation that students will complete at least some of the required course activities at other times such as reading the textbook, solving homework questions, or interacting with online resources. The advantage of these resources is that students can be engaged in learning activities at a time that might be more convenient for their schedule, like nights and weekends. However, the challenge with "out-of-class" activities is that students might not have access to help resources or personalized tutoring, and it is impossible to monitor all of their interactions. Out of class experiences could actually reinforce undesirable learning behaviors, like over-reliance on peers or web searches for information. Although online homework and tutoring systems are becoming increasingly sophisticated, many still emphasize getting the correct numerical result and may not provide much feedback on a student's problem solving process. Computer coaches will be reviewed further along with problem solving in Chapter 4. Additional general strategies are reviewed below.

One set of evidence-based practices is focused on gathering student responses that the instructor can use to plan instruction and respond to students' needs. For example, the strategy *Just-in-time Teaching* (JiTT) includes pre-class questions that students answer online prior to class, and then instructors adapt and fashion their instruction based on those responses (Novak et al., 1999). Some learning management systems include communication tools like discussion posts so instructors and students can ask and respond to questions. Students could also keep a reflective journal about what they learned and what questions they have about the material, which the instructor and/or teaching assistants can summarize and address with the whole class.

Another set of practices involve moving most of the basic content delivery from face-to-face classes to be online content viewed before class, sometimes referred to as a *flipped* classroom (see www.flipitphysics.com for an example). In that situation, more in-class time is devoted to collaborative activities like conceptual questions, or to refining students' understanding and developing problem solving skills. For example, students might complete online multimedia learning pre-lectures in conjunction with a course (Stelzer et al., 2010). These pre-lectures substitute for material that is traditionally communicated in lecture, and/or they could include additional things, like worked examples or quizzes for students to check their understanding; interestingly, students learn significantly more from interactive pre-lectures than from textbook presentations of the same material (Stelzer et al., 2009). Another advantage of video-based materials or animations is that students can periodically pause and rewind to revisit material while viewing it, letting them control the pace of instruction, and they can also revisit material again at a later time. Web-based modules like this with narrated animations have been shown to provide some increases in students' exam performance, but also improve students' attitudes toward a course (Sadaghiani, 2011; Stelzer et al., 2010).

5.1.5. Barriers to active learning instruction

According to a large-scale web survey of physics faculty teaching in the United States, nearly all faculty are familiar with one or more RBIS (or EBIPs) and several have implemented one at some point (Henderson & Dancy, 2007, 2009; Henderson et al., 2012). Approximately half indicate they are currently using at least one RBIS. Oftentimes the RBIS is substantially modified during implementation, which could impact the outcomes of instruction; nearly a third of adopters end up abandoning the RBIS altogether. When faculty discontinue using a particular RBIS, some of the reasons listed were that it did not seem to work (they did not see knowledge gains among students), it took up too much in-class time, students had a negative reaction to the approach, it was too cost-prohibitive to continue, and/or it was not supported by their department (Henderson & Dancy, 2009). Faculty might also be abandoning one approach in favor of trying out a different evidence-based instructional practice.

When a subset of faculty were interviewed and asked to elaborate on barriers to implementation, nearly all of them mentioned issues related to departmental norms and expectations of content coverage, lack of time to learn about and implement new approaches, and challenges with student attitudes or resistance toward aspects of the course (Henderson & Dancy, 2007). A smaller number cited structural constraints like the class size, room layout, and time structure of the course. In a separate analysis of this survey data, the use of innovative teaching strategies was found to be independent of the faculty member's age, type of institution, research productivity, and percentage of job related to teaching (Henderson *et al.*, 2012). Although faculty might hold *perceptions* that it is more challenging to implement innovative teaching at Ph.D.-granting institutions and it could potentially hurt their research productivity, this was not supported by research findings.

Students are also victims of their own perceptions—in fact, Chapter 6 discusses how students' perception of what works best for them in terms of learning run counter to measured outcomes. A recent study found that in active learning classes, students feel like they learned less, when in fact, they learned more than in a traditional style lecture class (Deslauriers *et al.*, 2019). This could lead to lower rates of student participation, and even lower evaluations at the end of a course (Gaffney & Gaffney, 2016). This underscores the need for faculty to explicitly talk about why the course is structured in a particular way and the values of active learning with their students. It is important to acknowledge that it might not always *feel* like they are learning more, but productively struggling with material leads to greater learning gains. A major exception to these findings is the introductory physics sequence for science and engineering majors at the University of Illinois, where the implementation of web-based pre-lectures, use of class time largely devoted to Peer Instruction, and a reduction of lecture time by 50 minutes per week, resulted in significantly improved student attitudes, better exam scores, and perceptions by students that the course was easier and that the lecture portion was more valuable when compared to when the course was taught traditionally (Stelzer *et al.*, 2010).

5.1.6. The use of Communities of Practice to encourage reformed instruction

Recent work investigating the use of EBIPs at the University of Illinois suggests a structure in which EBIPs can spread and thrive, which is in stark contrast to the barriers discussed above. The multi-year process leading to the spread of EBIPs at Illinois is documented in three publications (Herman *et al.*, 2018; Ma *et al.*, 2018; Mestre *et al.*, 2019). The catalyst for the reform was a grant from the National Science Foundation's Widening Implementation and Demonstration of Evidence-Based Reforms (WIDER) program. The WIDER project is not intended to promote the discovery of new knowledge but rather to explore adoption strategies for evidence-based reforms. Thirteen science and engineering departments across two colleges participated in the project. Each reform was centered around a team of faculty from the department consisting of faculty who agreed to work collaboratively on identifying and adopting an EBIP that met the context and need for an introductory course, to research its effectiveness once implemented, and to use the EBIP long-term by having different team members teach the introductory course over the years. Crucially, one WIDER principal investigator was embedded in each team and served as a mentor/resource to help the team identify and adopt an appropriate EBIP; the principal investigators possessed substantial pedagogical expertise that they shared with the departmental teams as needed.

A Communities of Practice (CoP) model (Wenger *et al.*, 2002) was used in the reform teams, with team members and mentor working collaboratively toward the common goal of adopting an EBIP to reform a large introductory course. The EBIP selected by each CoP was not prescribed but rather emerged from lengthy discussions over many weekly meetings held by the CoP, and was jointly "owned" by the CoP members and the department (department chair buy-in was required). Four EBIPs were predominantly adopted, namely flipped classrooms with pre-lectures, use of active learning with clickers, problem-based learning, and context-rich collaborative problem solving. In addition, a "teach the way you do research" mantra permeated the project, not only because research is something that professors at a research university understand well, but also to advertise to participating faculty that research into the effectiveness of a reform was the only way to determine its efficacy; further, this mantra served to dispense with proposed reforms based on individual team member's "hunches" on what worked best—the "evidence" in Evidence-Based Reforms dictated that any reform adopted had to have evidence that it worked. Various measures used in evaluating student performance indicated improved performance and higher student satisfaction following the reforms.

By the end of the 4-year project, the EBIPs adopted in the large "gateway" introductory science and engineering courses were impacting over 17,000 students per year. Additional research conducted by the WIDER principal investigators yielded some very interesting findings. In weekly meetings held by the principal investigators to discuss progress of the CoPs in which they were embedded, it was becoming clear that certain EBIPs were spreading across departments independent of the team's efforts. To study the spread of innovations, social network analyses were performed on survey data from all CoP faculty and it was found that the embedded mentors played a crucial role in the spread of innovations; the mentors often discussed what they learned in their weekly meetings about other reforms with the CoPs in which they were embedded, thereby facilitating dissemination.

There were several other indicators of both structural and cultural change:

- Faculty in the CoPs began publishing about their educational innovations. Over 50 peer reviewed publications emerged from 64 unique authors, 38 of which had never published education-related work. This was accomplished while these science and engineering faculty members maintained their own active research programs in their respective disciplines.
- CoP faculty submitted 21 external STEM education grant proposals (including WIDER itself), totaling over $22 million, with 8 being funded for a total of $6.0 million. There were 46 unique principal investigators in these proposals with 33 being STEM faculty (29 had never submitted an education-related proposal) and 13 being education faculty. Thus STEM faculty not only enjoyed their forays into educational reform, but enjoyed their collaborations with education faculty as well.
- Of the eleven CoPs, eight continued to operate after the WIDER project was over, suggesting that for the STEM faculty involved their education-related collaborations were treated similarly to their disciplinary collaborations.

5.2. What are the implications of research on active learning for instruction?

We offer the following implications of the research reviewed above for instruction:

- **Teaching by telling is ineffective for long-term learning and transfer.** The research reviewed in this chapter suggests that learning is not a spectator sport, as eloquently discussed in the National Research Council's publication,

How People Learn (2000). Passively listening to a lecture, no matter how polished, may provide the listener with an illusion of understanding but does little in terms of long term retention and ability to transfer the ideas covered in novel contexts. Instructors need to design learning experiences to be more "active" from both a cognitive and physical sense—traditional passive lectures result in lower student performance and higher failure rates (Freeman et al., 2014).

- **Traditional labs are not enough.** Some instructors might be thinking that students already participate in "active learning" instruction by doing hands-on laboratory activities. Research has shown that just being physically active with equipment does not ensure learning—students might be able to follow step-by-step instructions and fill in the blanks for "traditional" lab activities, but walk away with little understanding about what they did in an experiment and why, and about how to design experiments. Curricula need to make certain that students are cognitively engaged and thinking deeply about the material. Ideally, EBIPs should permeate all aspects of a course (lecture, laboratories, recitation/discussion sessions, assessments, etc.) and mesh together seamlessly to enhance student learning.
- **Assessment is critical.** At the very beginning of this book, we made a case for the importance of approaching classroom instruction in the same way we approach research—by systematically conducting investigations. If you are planning to implement one or more EBIPs, also devote some time to planning out how you will evaluate the effectiveness of instructional reforms. The Physics Education Research community has a wide selection of diagnostic tests and resources for assessing instruction.

- **Context is important.** Implementing evidence-based instructional practices takes significant effort and buy-in from instructors, and institutional barriers can quickly derail efforts. These barriers can include anything from a lack of support from administrators and/or colleagues, lack of facilities or financial resources and student resistance to reformed instruction.

5.3. Examples of teaching interventions based on learning research

Physics students could benefit from increased opportunities to discuss physics concepts with their peers during class, conduct meaningful laboratory experiments, and engage in practices to monitor their own learning. Some suggested instructional strategies are provided below.

- **Implement peer discussions about conceptually challenging questions.** Traditional physics instruction tends to focus on quantitative problem solving with little attention to students' qualitative understanding of concepts. Many EBIPs include opportunities for student–student discourse focused on students' ideas at multiple points in instruction. Earlier sections highlighted specific examples of this, such as Peer Instruction (Mazur, 1997) and Interactive Lecture Demonstrations (Sokoloff & Thornton, 1997, 2004). Also, simply having students talk to each other does not comprise an RBIS; having students discuss meaningful questions/problems that are within their reach is crucial to lasting learning, as well as instructor guidance. Chapter 2 included some examples of "clicker" questions to promote peer discussions and conceptual understanding.

- **Implement structured cooperative group work.** In conjunction with the first bullet, it is important to carefully structure group activities to promote interactivity and peer learning (Johnson et al., 1998). Whether students are discussing conceptual questions, conducting a laboratory experiment, or solving problems, there are classroom structures that can facilitate positive interactions. For example, it is important to design activities that blend positive interdependence (we sink or swim together) with individual accountability, foster social skills like communication and conflict management, and rotate roles within a group. Other research studies have found better results in problem solving with mixed ability groups and pairing up 2–3 women in a group instead of two men and one woman (Heller & Hollabaugh, 1992).
- **Structure laboratory experiences to reflect the processes of "doing science".** Although laboratory experiments have long been a part of physics instruction, the notion of engaging students in more authentic scientific practices started in the K-12 realm and is beginning to make its way into postsecondary education. Students benefit from practicing scientific skills like developing and using models, planning and carrying out investigations, analyzing and interpreting data, and constructing explanations (NRC, 2012a). This chapter reviewed several laboratory curricula that break the traditional format of "cookbook labs" and provide increased opportunities for students to make decisions and figure things out for themselves.
- **Implement formative assessment classroom techniques to monitor student learning and inform instruction.** Research indicates how prior knowledge plays a key role in the process of learning (NRC, 2000). Instructors need to be aware of students' pre-existing ideas and design lessons to

elicit and build on scientifically correct ideas, and to help remedy stubborn misconceptions. This chapter explored a variety of strategies for making students' learning more visible before, during, and after instruction using formative assessment classroom techniques (Keeley, 2008). Some of these techniques are enhanced by using technology like classroom response systems or online assessment tools. More strategies for using assessment in the service of learning are provided in Chapter 7.
- **Implement diagnostic assessments to evaluate students' knowledge, skills, and attitudes.** If you are currently using or planning to use reformed instructional strategies, it is helpful to collect evidence of student learning and attitudes to better evaluate the effectiveness of the implementation (and/or track multiple reform efforts). The Physics Education Research community has developed a host of assessment resources and tools for evaluating students' conceptual knowledge, attitudes and beliefs, scientific reasoning skills, and problem solving skills (see https://www.physport.org/Assessment.cfm). As Chapter 6 will discuss, effective learning strategies are counterintuitive for many students who have erroneous notions of what works best for them.

References

Bandura, A. (1986). *Social Foundations of Thought and Action: A Social Cognitive Theory.* Englewood Cliffs, NJ: Prentice-Hall.

Beichner, R.J. (2008). The SCALE-UP project: A student-centered active learning environment for undergraduate programs. Paper presented at the National Research Council's Workshop on Evidence on Promising Practices in Undergraduate Science, Technology, Engineering, and Mathematics Education, Washington, DC. http://sites.nationalacademies.org/DBASSE/BOSE/DBASSE_071087

Bruner, J. S. (1961). The act of discovery. *Harvard Educational Review*, **31**(1), 21–32.

Chappuis, J. (2015). *Seven Strategies of Assessment for Learning*, 2nd Ed. New York: Pearson Education.

Christian, W. & Belloni, M. (2003). *Physlet Physics: Interactive Illustrations, Explorations, and Problems for Introductory Physics*. Upper Saddle River, NJ: Prentice-Hall.

Crouch, C.H., Fagan, A.P., Callan, J.P. & Mazur, E. (2004). Classroom demonstrations: Learning tools or entertainment? *American Journal of Physics*, **72**(6), 835–838. https://doi.org/10.1119/1.1707018

Crouch, C.H. & Mazur, E. (2001). Peer Instruction: Ten years of experience and results. *American Journal of Physics*, **69**(9), 970–977. https://doi.org/10.1119/1.1374249

Cummings, K. (2011). A developmental history of Physics Education Research. Commissioned paper by the National Academies Board on Science Education on Status, Contributions, and Future Directions of Discipline-Based Education Research (DBER), Washington, DC. [http://sites.nationalacademies.org/DBASSE/BOSE/DBASSE_071087]

Dancy, M. & Henderson, C. (2007). Framework for articulating instructional practices and conceptions. *Physical Review Special Topics – Physics Education Research*, **3**(010103). https://doi.org/10.1103/PhysRevSTPER.3.010103

Deslauriers, L., McCarty, L.S., Miller, K., Callaghan, K. & Kestin, G. (2019). Measuring actual learning versus feeling of learning in response to being actively engaged in the classroom. *Proceedings of the National Academy of Sciences of the United States of America*, **116**(39), 19251–19257. https://doi.org/10.1073/pnas.1821936116

Docktor, J.L. & Mestre, J.P. (2014). Synthesis of discipline-based education research in physics. *Physical Review Special Topics – Physics Education Research*, **10**(020119). https://doi.org/10.1103/PhysRevSTPER.10.020119

Dufresne, R.J., Gerace, W.J., Leonard, W.J., Mestre, J.P. & Wenk, L. (1996). Classtalk: A classroom communication system for active learning,

Journal of Computing in Higher Education, **7**(2), 3–47. http://dx.doi.org/10.1007/BF02948592

Etkina, E. & Van Heuvelen, A. (2001). Investigative Science Learning Environment: Using the processes of science and cognitive strategies to learn physics. *Proceedings of the 2001 Physics Education Research Conference*. Rochester, NY, pp. 17–21.

Etkina, E. & Van Heuvelen, A. (2006). *The Physics Active Learning Guide*. San Francisco, CA: Addison Wesley.

Freeman, S., Eddy, S.L., McDonough, M., Smith, M.K., Okoroafor, N., Jordt, H. & Wenderoth, M.P. (2014). Active learning increases student performance in science, engineering, and mathematics. *Proceedings of the National Academy of Sciences of the United States of America*, **111**(23), 8410–8415. https://doi.org/10.1073/pnas.1319030111

Gaffney, J.D.H. & Gaffney, A.L.H. (2016). Student satisfaction in interactive engagement-based physics classes. *Physical Review Physics Education Research*, **12**(020125). https://doi.org/10.1103/PhysRevPhysEducRes.12.020125

Gaffney, J.D.H., Richards, E., Bridget Kustusch, M. Ding, L. & Beichner, R.J. (2008). Scaling up educational reform. *Journal of College Science Teaching*, **37**(5), 48–53.

Hake, R.R. (1998). Interactive-engagement versus traditional methods: A six-thousand student survey of mechanics test data for introductory physics courses. *American Journal of Physics*, **66**(1), 64–74. http://dx.doi.org/10.1119/1.18809

Heller, P., Keith, R. & Anderson, S. (1992). Teaching problem solving through cooperative grouping. Part 1:Group versus individual problem solving. *American Journal of Physics*, **60**(7), 627–636. https://doi.org/10.1119/1.17117

Heller, P. & Hollabaugh, M. (1992). Teaching problem solving through cooperative grouping. Part 2: Designing problems and structuring groups. *American Journal Physics*, **60**(7), 637–644. https://doi.org/10.1119/1.17118

Henderson, C. & Dancy, M.H. (2007). Barriers to the use of research-based instructional strategies: The influence of both individual and situational characteristics. *Physical Review Special Topics – Physics Education Research*, **3**(020102). https://doi.org/10.1103/PhysRevSTPER.3.020102

Henderson, C. & Dancy, M.H. (2009). Impact of physics education research on the teaching of introductory quantitative physics in the United States. *Physical Review Special Topics – Physics Education Research*, **5**(020107). https://doi.org/10.1103/PhysRevSTPER.5.020107

Henderson, C., Dancy, M. & Niewiadomska-Bugaj, M. (2012). Use of research-based instructional strategies in physics: Where do faculty leave the innovation-decision process? *Physical Review Special Topics – Physics Education Research*, **8**(020104). https://doi.org/10.1103/PhysRevSTPER.8.020104

Herman, G.L., Greene, J.C., Hahn, L.D., Mestre, J.P., West, M. & Tomkin, J. H. (2018). Changing the teaching culture in introductory STEM courses at a large research university. *Journal of College Science Teaching*, **47**(6), 32–38.

Johnson, D.W., Johnson, R.T. & Holubec, E.J. (1998). *Cooperation in the Classroom 7th Ed.* Edina, MN: Interaction Book Company.

Keeley, P.D. (2008). *Science Formative Assessment: 75 Practical Strategies for Linking Assessment, Instruction, and Learning.* NSTA Press.

Laws, P. (2004). *Workshop Physics Activity Guide Vol. 1-4.* New York: Wiley and Sons.

Lyman, F. (1981). The responsive classroom discussion: The inclusion of all students. In A.S. Anderson (Ed.), *Mainstreaming Digest*, pp. 109–113. College Park, MD: University of Maryland College of Education.

Ma, S., Herman, G.L., West, M., Tomkin, J. & Mestre, J. (2019) Studying STEM Faculty communities of practice through social network analysis. *The Journal of Higher Education*, **90**(5), 773–799. doi: 10.1080/00221546.2018.1557100

Mazur, E. (1997). *Peer Instruction: A User's Manual.* Upper Saddle River, NJ: Prentice Hall.

McDaniel, M.A., Stoen, S.M., Frey, R.F., Markow, Z.E., Hynes, K.M., Zhao, J. & Cahill, M.J. (2016). Dissociative conceptual and quantitative problem solving outcomes across interactive engagement and traditional format introductory physics. *Physical Review Physics Education Research*, **12**(020141).

McDermott, L. Schaffer, P. & the Physics Education Group at the University of Washington (2002). *Tutorials in Introductory Physics*. Upper Saddle River, NJ: Prentice Hall.

Meltzer, D.E. & Otero, V.K. (2015). A brief history of physics education in the United States. *American Journal of Physics*, **83**(5), 447–458. https://doi.org/10.1119/1.4902397

Meltzer, D.E. & Thornton, R.K. (2012). Resource Letter ALIP-1: Active-learning instruction in Physics. *American Journal of Physics*, **80**(6), 478–496. https://doi.org/10.1119/1.3678299

Mestre, J.P. (2001). Implications of research on learning for the education of prospective science and physics teachers. *Physics Education*, **36**(44), 44–51. https://iopscience.iop.org/article/10.1088/0031-9120/36/1/308/pdf

Mestre, J.P., Herman, G.L., Tomkin, J.H. & West, M. (2019). Keep your friends close and your colleagues nearby: The hidden ties that improve STEM education. *Change: The Magazine of Higher Learning*, **51**(1), 42–49.

Morphew, J.W. & Mestre, J.P. (2018). Exploring the connection between problem solving and conceptual understanding in physics. *Revista de Enseñanza de la Física*, **30**(2), 75–85.

National Research Council (2000). *How People Learn: Brain, Mind, Experience, and School: Expanded Edition*. Washington, DC: The National Academies Press. https://doi.org/10.17226/9853

National Research Council (2012a). *A Framework for K-12 Science Education: Practices, Crosscutting Concepts, and Core Ideas*. Washington, DC: The National Academies Press. https://doi.org/10.17226/13165

National Research Council (2012b). *Discipline-Based Education Research: Understanding and Improving Learning in Undergraduate Science and Engineering*. Washington, DC: The National Academies Press. https://doi.org/10.17226/13362

National Research Council (2013). *Adapting to a Changing World – Challenges and Opportunities in Undergraduate Physics Education.* Washington, DC: The National Academies Press.

Novak, G.M., Patterson, E.T., Gavrin, A. D. & Christian, W. (1999). *Just-in-time Teaching: Blending Active Learning with Web Technology.* Upper Saddle River, NJ: Prentice Hall.

Redish, E.F. (2003). *Teaching Physics with the Physics Suite.* New York: Wiley.

Sadaghiani, H.R. (2011). Using multimedia learning modules in a hybrid-online course in electricity and magnetism. *Physical Review Special Topics – Physics Education Research*, **7**(010102). https://doi.org/10.1103/PhysRevSTPER.7.010102

Schwartz, D.L. & Bransford, J.D. (1998) A Time For Telling. *Cognition and Instruction*, **16**(4), 475–5223. doi: 10.1207/s1532690xci1604_4

Smith, M.K., Wood, W.B., Adams, W.K., Wieman, C., Knight, J.K., Guild, N. & Su, T.T. (2009). Why peer discussion improves student performance on in-class concept questions. *Science*, **323**(5910), 122–124. http://dx.doi.org/10.1126/science.1165919

Sokoloff, D.R. & Thornton, R.K. (1997). Using interactive lecture demonstrations to create an active learning environment. *The Physics Teacher*, **35**(6), 340–347.

Sokoloff, D.R. & Thornton R.K. (2004). *Interactive Lecture Demonstrations: Active Learning In Introductory Physics.* New York: John Wiley & Sons.

Sokoloff, D.R., Thornton, R.K. & Laws, P.W. (2004). *RealTime Physics: Active Learning Laboratories* (2nd ed.) *Module 1: Mechanics, Module 2: Heat and Thermodynamics, Module 3: Electric Circuits, Module 4: Light and Optics.* Hoboken, NJ: John Wiley & Sons.

Stelzer, T., Brookes, D.T., Gladding, G. & Mestre, J.P. (2010). Impact of multimedia learning modules on an introductory course on electricity and magnetism. *American Journal of Physics*, **78**(7), 755–759. https://doi.org/10.1119/1.3369920

Stelzer, T., Gladding, G., Mestre, J.P. & Brookes, D.T. (2009). Comparing the efficacy of multimedia modules with traditional textbooks for learning introductory physics content. *American Journal of Physics*, **77**(2), 184–190.

Van Heuvelen, A., and Etkina, E. (2006). *The Physics Active Learning Guide*. San Francisco, CA: Pearson, Addison Wesley.

Vygotsky, L.S. (1978). *Mind in Society: The Development of the Higher Psychological Processes*. Cambridge, MA: The Harvard University Press. (Originally published 1930, New York: Oxford University Press.)

Wenger, E., McDermott, R. & Snyder, W. M. (2002). *Cultivating Communities of Practice*. Cambridge, MA: Harvard Business Press.

Wilson, J. (1994). The CUPLE physics studio. *Physics Teacher*, **32**, 518–523. http://dx.doi.org/10.1119/1.2344100

Zhang, P., Ding, L. & Mazur, E. (2017). Peer Instruction in introductory physics: A method to bring about positive changes in students' attitudes and beliefs. *Physical Review Physics Education Research*, **13**(010104), 1–9. https://doi.org/10.1103/PhysRevPhysEducRes.13.010104

Chapter

6 Students' Perceptions of Learning and their Study Habits

6.1. What does research on students' perceptions of learning and studying tell us?

We as instructors have a direct influence on students during those times that we are in contact with them, such as during class and office hours. We also have some indirect influence on students. For example, the tests we administer and the homework we assign send messages to students about what we think is important in a course, and students interpret and act on those messages since they want to do well in our courses. However, most of the learning that students do takes place outside of our direct influence. Students study on their own, take tests on their own and (mostly) do homework on their own. During those types of "learning episodes" students make judgments and decisions about how to optimize learning. However, as the research reviewed in this chapter will point out, those judgments and decisions quite often run counter to research evidence on optimizing learning in ways that result in long-term retention and in ability to apply the learning to novel contexts (i.e., transfer). The research we will review in this chapter largely comes from cognitive and educational psychology and was not carried out within a physics context, or a science context for that matter. But the findings below have generalizability and carry important implications for how to structure our courses to help students optimize their learning. We will discuss those implications as well as suggest ways of using those implications to students' benefit.

6.1.1. Research on study strategies

We begin with a discussion of study habits used by students. The findings that we will review are very nicely summarized in two reports (Dunlosky *et al.*, 2013; Pashler *et al.*, 2007). These reports reviewed and synthesized hundreds of studies in order to identify both students' study habits and instructional techniques that held promise for student learning. What will become clear is that quite often students' perception of effective study strategies are not borne out by research findings, while other study habits that are deemed ineffectual by students are in fact quite effective. There are also some "mixed" findings in that certain study habits preferred by students are actually very effective but with important caveats that render them mediocre at best.

Let us start by dispensing with some ineffective study techniques. A very popular technique among students, but among the least effective, is *highlighting/underlining* text. Many of us who have visited our campus' bookstore and browsed some of the used textbooks for sale have noticed that most have highlighting, ranging from sparse to dense highlighting. Highlighting/underlining is a "feel good" strategy that helps students build *familiarity* with the material but does little to develop *competence* with the material. In physics, being able to apply concepts in multiple contexts is key to success, and highlighting does little to develop the needed skills. Two other techniques earning low effectiveness for similar reasons are *rereading* and *summarizing*. As with highlighting, both are good for helping students develop familiarity with the material, which unfortunately students confuse with competence (more on this in the next chapter on assessment). When students study, they need to make some decision about when they have studied enough, and these three techniques build considerable familiarity with the material leading to shallow learning, and unfortunately, to students judging that they are well-prepared; when students who use these techniques walk into an exam, everything will look familiar, but that does not translate into being able to apply concepts to solve problems.

Note a common feature of the three ineffective study strategies described in the previous paragraph: They are easy to implement and require minimal effort. The more successful learning strategies require more effort on the part of the learner—physical effort in the case of sports, mental efforts in the case of academic subjects. Robert Bjork, a psychologist at UCLA who studies learning and memory, refers to creating "desirable difficulties" in order to promote lasting learning that transfers (Bjork, 1994; Bjork & Bjork, 2014; Schmidt & Bjork, 1992). He argues that adding a certain type of difficulty to tasks forces learners to notice and store away in memory subtleties that would otherwise have been missed. The term "desirable" is crucial in the descriptor since simply adding difficulty to a task accomplishes little other than frustrating the learner—for example, giving students a very difficult physics problem to solve right after covering a major topic but before the student has had a chance to "explore the space" and develop competencies. A desirable difficulty is making a task harder when the learner possesses all the tools needed to make progress. Study strategies that have been shown to be effective contain desirable difficulties, although some evidence exists that desirable difficulties differentially benefit high-ability students more than low-ability students (Wenzel & Reinhard, 2019). The notion of desirable difficulties is similar to *productive struggle* in mathematics instruction (Hiebert & Grouws, 2007). Rather than immediately rushing to help students when they are unsure about how to proceed, giving them some time to wrestle with a problem on their own while providing minimal scaffolding can promote the development of grit and a growth mindset.

One successful study strategy is *distributed practice*, or *spaced practice*. Perhaps the best example of distributed practice is to space studying for an exam over several sessions, rather than "massed practice" which consists of doing all the studying at once just before the exam. Note that massed practice, otherwise known as cramming, seems to be the method preferred by students when preparing for an exam. It should be pointed out that cramming is not without its virtues, otherwise students would have abandoned the practice long ago. Massed practice is very valuable for retaining information for regurgitation right after the cramming session—at the time of the exam. Students often feel rewarded for their efforts following an "all-nighter" after noting a respectable grade on a test. However, studies consistently reveal that massed practice is very *ineffective* for learning that lasts (Dunlosky *et al.*, 2013; Pashler *et al.*, 2007; Schmidt & Bjork, 1992). Studies comparing groups of students, where one group distributes study over time and one group masses study (equating for total study time) find that the massed practice group slightly outperforms the distributed practice group on a test administered immediately after cramming, but on a delayed test administered one week later, the pattern reverses, with those using distributed practice significantly outperforming those who cram. It seems that this finding should be plastered all over university dorms, academic buildings and dining commons! Granted, cramming strategies may not be chosen willingly by students, but may be a default strategy. Students are pressed for time, with deadlines looming in every course, and so studying at the last minute is one way of coping with lack of organizational skills. However, taking the "distributed practice medicine" seems very advisable since in the long run, it is a time-saver for such things as studying later for a cumulative final exam, for retaining and transferring knowledge for later use in one's major, and for reaping the most benefit from a very expensive college education. What makes adoption of this strategy difficult for students is that they have empirical evidence that cramming works (their performance in an exam immediately after cramming is respectable), although that evidence is incomplete and flawed.

Another effective study strategy with desirable difficulty is *interleaved practice*. Interleaved practice consists of varying practice across different types of items or activities. In stark contrast is *blocked practice*, consisting of practicing the same type of item or activity. To use a sports analogy, for someone learning to play tennis, after being introduced to different strokes and playing tennis for some period of time (e.g., weeks), the player would show more improvement in their overall game, if in practice sessions, they varied the strokes they practiced; for example, mixing forehands, backhands and serves in every practice session. Studies have shown that there is more improvement with this type of practice than spending the same practice time blocking strokes, for example, practicing only backhands in one session, only serves in another, and so on. In physics, as in just about every academic discipline, instruction is geared around blocked practice. The chapters in a textbook are arranged by topics, with exercises and problems at the back of each chapter dealing with the topic of that chapter. Homework assignments are also structured as blocked practice, with each homework set containing problems from the last chapter or lectures covered. A student opening a homework assignment therefore knows that the particular assignment will deal with energy or momentum concepts, for example. Further, although exam content is partially interleaved, dealing with the topics covered in the last three or so weeks of a course, typical semester exams are blocked, covering a small number of topics. With rare exceptions, the only time when students are forced to perform interleaved practice is during a cumulative final exam. The reader can likely predict the instructional strategies that we will recommend later in this chapter, which would blend interleaved practice throughout a course, adding desirable difficulties for students and some extra work for the instructor in implementing this structural change. In short, interleaved practice allows students to differentiate which concepts apply to which contexts.

A form of interleaved practice is also recommended in the report by Pashler *et al.* (2007) namely to interleave worked-out examples with problem solving exercises. There is a substantial literature on the use of worked examples as a means of teaching problem solving ((Sweller & Cooper, 1985; Ward & Sweller, 1990; Pashler *et al.*, 2007) and references therein). Generally the dual benefits of studying worked examples are that they exhibit correct paths to solutions, as opposed to students taking incorrect paths and thereby reinforcing an incorrect approach, and that studying worked examples take less time than solving problems on one's own—for example, a student can likely study three worked examples in the same time as it might take them to solve a single problem on their own. Student engagement in studying worked examples is a confounding factor, however—reading a worked example with all the steps shown is typically easy to follow but the mental processing needed to follow a solution is considerably less than that needed to internalize the solution so that the learner can reproduce it. Therefore adding desirable difficulties in studying worked examples, such as leaving out steps or asking deep questions along the way, helps the student to internalize the solution better than passive reading of the worked example. Providing worked examples at the right level is also important since a worked solution for too difficult a problem may not be understood by a student, and a worked solution to too easy a problem will bore the student and serve little purpose. One virtue of interleaving worked examples with problem solving exercises is that a student may become stuck when attempting to solve a problem, then by reading an isomorphic worked example, realize what was hampering progress in the problem that they were attempting to solve.

Two additional effective study strategies discussed in the Pashler *et al.* report are worthy of mention, although for reasons we will discuss, are better categorized as effective instructional strategies. The first is asking and answering deep questions. This would be a great study strategy if only beginning students, who are novices in physics, were able to ask and answer deep questions on their own. Previous research has shown, for example, that when provided with a physics scenario students are inept at posing meaningful problems from the scenario (Mestre, 2002). Therefore the "asking" part of asking and answering deep questions needs to be provided by instructors. The first two components of strategy writing as discussed in Chapter 3, namely identifying the major principle(s) needed to solve a problem and providing a justification for why the principle(s) apply in that particular instance, are examples of asking/answering deep questions.

The second instructional strategy is to combine abstract and concrete representations of concepts. This is common practice in teaching physics, although perhaps not done extensively enough. When instructors and textbooks introduce a new abstract concept, it is followed by illustrations of ways of applying the concept to solve problems. Leaving out concrete examples would render the concept a mere abstraction with no anchor to the physical world. Equally important is to provide enough concrete cases where the concept can be applied, as well as cases where it does not apply in order to promote transfer (i.e., the flexible and appropriate application of the concept, see, for example, (Mestre, 2005)). Combining abstraction with concreteness, together with appropriate and inappropriate contexts in which to apply a concept, helps to build and refine a students' knowledge base in memory. For example, suppose that after introducing conservation of mechanical energy, an instructor presents a single sample problem to find the speed of a block at the bottom of a curved ramp. Recall from Chapter 3 that novices tend to focus on surface attributes, not on deep structure. If this is all the student sees, it is highly likely that s/he will assume that conservation of mechanical energy is applicable only to blocks on curved ramps. Many of us have noticed that after covering conservation of mechanical energy, giving students a problem where a block is released from the top of a straight, frictionless ramp results in them applying Newton's Second Law since that situation is associated with that concept, as opposed to the easier conservation of mechanical energy.

6.1.2. What are the actual patterns of learning and forgetting?

Psychologists have been working to develop a model of learning and memory for at least one hundred years, but many of those models were based on remembering nonsense syllables or words and did not take place in the context of a classroom (Ebbinghaus, 1913). In the past, the term "learning curve" typically referred to the observation that with a repetitive task, the time to complete the task decreased according to a power law function (Newell & Rosenbloom, 1980). Most graphical representations of classroom learning are based on either an exponential rise in learning that occurs as a result of instruction or an "S-curve" modeled as a logistic sigmoid function (Mitchell, 1997). In an S-curve model (see Fig. 6.1), acquisition of knowledge starts with small steps, then becomes larger steps, and reduces to successfully smaller ones as learning reaches some maximum or limit on a topic. After the learning reaches a maximum then with

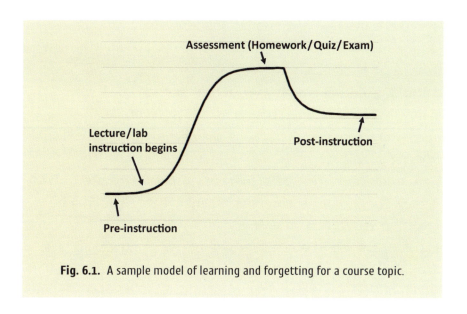

Fig. 6.1. A sample model of learning and forgetting for a course topic.

time a forgetting curve takes over as an exponential decay or power law decay to some new value. A sample smooth graph of this process is presented (Fig. 6.1), however actual student learning might be much more stepwise. Time scales can vary widely from hours to days and even years depending on the context.

Heckler and Sayre (2010) examined students' responses to questions about electricity and magnetism at multiple time points throughout an introductory physics course. They found an increase in student performance once lecture and laboratory instruction began on a particular topic, and it peaked approximately one week later when online homework was due. Most students completed their online homework within two days of the deadline and received immediate feedback on their responses. After the homework deadline, performance on the questions decreased rapidly within a matter of a few days after the deadline (Sayre & Heckler, 2009). The shape of the learning and forgetting curves varied by topic; sometimes there was a sharp exponential or stepwise increase just prior to the assessment and sometimes performance did not exhibit such a rapid decline after the assessment. A study looking at Newton's Third Law saw an increase in learning during the unit on forces that declined during the energy unit, but rebounded again once students learned about momentum and the interactions that happen during collisions (Sayre et al., 2012).

A study comparing an activity-based physics course to traditionally taught course observed different decay patterns in the forgetting curve (Franklin et al., 2014). The researchers found that both groups of students saw a nearly identical increase in learning with instruction, however, the students in the traditionally taught course saw a rapid decline in performance after the exam, returning back to their pre-instruction levels after three weeks. The students in the activity-based course maintained their level of performance or even exceeded it as they learned new topics. This helps to explain why courses reformed to include active learning often exhibit higher overall pre-post learning gains on a concept inventory test even though the short-term learning might be similar to traditionally taught courses.

In addition to learning and forgetting, studies have also found that the phenomenon of *interference* can impact learning of a topic. For example, immediately after learning about electric force students can correctly determine the direction of a force on a charged particle on an electric field, but incorrectly apply these ideas to particles in magnetic fields (Scaife & Heckler, 2011). After learning about magnetic fields they correct their ideas, but then incorrectly apply the force direction from a magnetic field to electric fields. Another study found that after students learned about electric potential, this information interfered with their ability to correctly answer questions about the vector nature of electric fields (Sayre & Heckler, 2009). These examples illustrate the complex nature of learning and patterns of learning and decay in a course.

How can we structure a course to address the rapid decline in memory that typically happens after an assessment (a so-called brain dump or mind wipe)? The research reviewed in this section suggests that research-based instructional strategies or instruction that promotes active learning (see Chapter 5) can improve long-term retention of information. The use of categorization tasks or concept mapping can help students see the "big picture" of topics in a physics course and the conditions under which those concepts and principles are applicable. In the problem solving chapter (Chapter 4) we described the idea of synthesis problems that combine the use of multiple principles separated in the timescale of a course, however scaffolding was needed to assist students with solving those problems. Other strategies to improve retention include distributed practice rather than massed practice/cramming and frequent testing for students to receive feedback on their performance (see Chapter 7). In addition, designing assessments that require students to apply information from previous chapters or units can reinforce the importance of retaining this information.

6.1.3. Students' metacognition about studying and learning

Thus far we have discussed effective study (and instructional) strategies emerging from hundreds of cognitive and educational psychology studies outside of physics. We have not discussed the decisions students make about studying. When students study, they make internal decisions that impact learning. For example, how does a student decide when they have studied enough, or learned enough, to put studying aside? These types of decisions fall under the broad category of *metacognition*, which loosely defined means thinking about, and regulating, one's own thought processes. We next discuss students' metacognition about studying and learning, and as we will see, students often fool themselves into thinking that they have studied or learned enough only to do poorly in an exam they prepared for.

In studying, students must decide what to study, how to study, and how long to study. Consciously or subconsciously students perform metacognitive monitoring in order to decide what they need to study, and when they can stop studying. Such monitoring evaluates one's current knowledge against some set of criteria imposed by the learner and the context. It is important to note that these processes are largely subjective—for example, we discussed earlier in this chapter how students often mistake familiarity or fluency with the material with competence with the material, and so if familiarity/fluency is an important criterion to be satisfied, a student may stop studying long before she or he evaluates competence with the material (e.g., by taking an old test under exam conditions). Unfortunately, studies have shown that the fluency with which an item is retrieved from memory impacts learners' metacognitive judgments of learning (Ackerman & Zalmanov, 2012; Koriat & Ma'ayan, 2005). For example, individuals predicting their ability to recall answers from a general knowledge test will often judge those items they answered fastest as most accurate whereas accuracy of recall is higher for items that take longer to answer (Benjamin et al., 1998). This is particularly relevant for physics courses where common misconceptions are often fluently retrieved. A more subtle distinction between two types of fluency should also be mentioned. Fluency with which a problem solution is generated by the student is desirable and aligned with the student's study goals. On the other hand, fluency in reading a worked solution is misleading since the student is good at reading (and likely following the solution), but it is not clear that the student would be able to generate the solution on their own later.

In order to make a sound decision on when to stop studying, the student's estimate of their knowledge and skills must closely match their actual level of knowledge and skills (Ariel et al., 2009; Metcalf & Kornell, 2005). However, for many students the study techniques that they employ are not conducive to reach the mastery they desire. For example, students erroneously believe that blocked and massed practices are more beneficial than interleaved and distributed practices (Schmidt & Bjork, 1992). Another strong erroneous belief by students is that adding more study sessions is more effective at preparing for an exam than taking practice tests similar to those they are preparing to take (Kornell & Son, 2009), even though using a test to judge learning is an objective and more accurate measure of learning (see Chapter 7 for additional research on this). One would think that exam performance would be the best indicator of whether or not a student is using successful study habits, but unfortunately research indicates that students tend to ignore this evidence and keep using the same study strategies throughout a semester regardless of whether or not exam performance suggests otherwise (Blasiman *et al.*, 2017).

In studying the accuracy of students' metacognitive monitoring, a very common paradigm is to ask a learner to make judgments about their learning at various points in the learning process, and two types of judgments used are *judgments of learning* (JOL) and *retrospective confidence judgments* (RCJ) (Dunlosky & Thiede, 2013). JOLs are made after studying but before the learner is tested on the learned material, while RCJs are made after the learner is tested on the material. For example, a JOL might consist of asking students to rate on a scale of 1–10 how well-prepared they think they are in an exam they are about to take (or what grade they think they will earn), and an RCJ might consist of asking students to rate on a scale of 1–10 how well they think they performed immediately after taking the exam (or what grade they think they received on the exam that they just completed). Findings reveal that accurate JOLs and RCJs in a task are directly related to the learner's ability to accurately perform that task (Ehrlinger *et al.*, 2008; Handel & Dresel, 2018; Handel & Fritzsche, 2016; Kelemen *et al.*, 2007; Kruger & Dunning, 1999; Rebello, 2012; Schneider, 2002); another way of putting it is that when students' self-awareness of their level of learning is accurate, they tend to do well on the task they had prepared for. What is perhaps most insidious is the finding that low-performing students are less accurate in their metacognitive judgments as measured by JOLs and RCJs; low-performers not only think they are better prepared when walking into a test than they actually are, but also think they performed above average even after taking the test. In short, low-performers are grossly overconfident in their preparation and fail to recognize that they did poorly on an exam even after taking it. In contrast, high-performers are often slightly under-confident as measured by JOLs when walking into an exam and think they did slightly worse than their actual performance as measured by RCJs (Dunning *et al.*, 2003; Griffin *et al.*, 2009; Schlosser *et al.*, 2013; Shake & Schulley, 2014). This has led to low-performing students being portrayed as suffering from a "double-curse," as eloquently described in the following quote:

> *"In many significant social and intellectual domains, the skills necessary to recognize competence are extremely close if not identical to those needed to produce competent responses. ... Thus, incompetent individuals suffer a double curse: Their deficits cause them to make errors and also prevent them from gaining insight into their errors. Several studies have now shown that incompetent individuals (i.e., those performing poorly relative to their peers) fail to show much insight into just how deficient their performance is (Kruger & Dunning, 1999). ... College students scoring in the bottom 25% on a course exam walked out of the exam room thinking that they outperformed a majority of their peers (Dunning, Johnson, Ehrlinger, & Kruger, 2003). Compared with good students, poor students less successfully identify which specific questions they have gotten right on an exam and which they have gotten wrong (Sinkavich, 1995)."*
>
> *(Dunning, Johnson, Ehrlinger & Kruger, 2003, pp. 73–74)*

Most of us have experienced students coming to our offices and lamenting poor performance in an exam despite being "A" students and spending considerable time studying for the exam; when we probe their study strategies, we often find the pattern described above (i.e., study strategies that build familiarity, not competence, and poor judgments of learning), which does little to build the competence needed to apply physics knowledge and procedures to solve problems. This is a difficult problem to solve since evidence also suggests that providing underperforming students with feedback showing them that their judgments of learning are highly inaccurate compared to actual exam performance does little to help better calibrate future judgments (Morphew, 2019).

6.2. What are the implications of research into students' view of learning and studying for instruction?

We offer the following implications of the research reviewed above for instruction:

- **Students' perceptions of good study strategies run counter to research evidence.** Common study strategies favored by students to prepare for exams, such as highlighting or underlining text, re-reading notes and course material, and summarizing, build familiarity and fluency with the material to be learned, not competence. These study strategies require minimal effort and yield minimal payoff. In a complex domain like physics learning concepts and how they are applied to solve problems are crucial to success, but study strategies that build familiarity with concepts do little to help students learn what concepts to apply, when to apply them, and procedures for applying them across a variety of contexts.

- **Effective study strategies contain "desirable difficulties" that require more effort and deeper processing of the to-be-learned material on the part of the student.** Effective study strategies, such as spaced/distributed practice (in contrast to massed practice or cramming), interleaved practice (in contrast to blocked practice), and asking/answering deep questions, offer more promise for learning that lasts. Unfortunately, these strategies are not commonly used by students in studying or by instructors in structuring their courses.
- **Students who do poorly on tests do little to change their study habits.** Research indicates that even when faced with evidence that their study habits are ineffective for exam preparation, poorly performing students keep the same study habits but simply add more study time in an effort to remedy the situation. More study time using ineffective study strategies does little to improve performance. If students knew more effective learning strategies they may be more likely to adopt them.
- **Students use subjective judgments in deciding when to stop studying for an exam, when objective judgments would serve them better.** Students tend to judge readiness for an exam when they reach a certain level of familiarity with the material, instead of competence with the material. More subjective measures of exam preparation, such as taking an old exam under exam conditions, are seldom used by students, when such measures are more accurate measures of preparation, and in addition, would help students target their studying by focusing on topics and problem types that they get wrong.
- **Judgments of learning by poorly performing students are grossly overestimated.** Poorly performing students

overestimate the grade they will earn on an exam both before, and after taking the exam, and providing feedback on their miscalibration does not remedy the situation. Researchers posit that the skills needed to make accurate judgments of learning are the same as those needed to perform well on exams, making the development of intervention strategies to help underperforming students challenging.

6.3. Examples of teaching interventions based on learning research

Research on students' study habits and judgments of learning suggest that we can both, help students change some of their study habits to improve learning, and coordinate instruction in support of better study habits. The most difficult nut to crack is the finding that poorly performing students have an inflated view of their subject matter understanding, and further that providing them evidence of their miscalibration does little to improve it (Miller & Geraci, 2011a, 2011b; Morphew, 2019). Nevertheless, there are some steps that can be taken to curb ineffective student study behaviors and to improve instruction based on the findings reviewed in this chapter.

- **Summarize for students early in a course the salient research findings on effective studying.** Making students aware of both effective (e.g., distributed practice, objective measures of learning like taking practice tests) and ineffective (e.g., cramming, only reviewing course notes and previous homework before an exam) study habits could help them curb bad habits. Although students will very likely be hesitant to change study habits that work well in most of their other courses, telling them early on that physics is unforgiving if not learned at a deep level (e.g., understanding concepts and problem-solving procedures and how to apply them across contexts) will "read into the record" what is needed to do well in the course. After the first exam's grades are returned to students and many come to see us to ask how they can do better, we can refer back to the summary we provided to them of effective study habits and analyze the study habits they used to study for the exam, as well as offer alternatives to their study habits. Another strategy to support this reflection is using a written *exam wrapper* which prompts students to explicitly write down how they studied for the most recent exam and what they will do differently to prepare for the next exam (Ambrose et al., 2010). This also helps to place the onus of learning on the student rather than blaming the instructor for writing an exam that was "unfair" or too hard in their view.

- **Make old exams available for students to gauge their preparation for exams.** Point out to students that taking old exams *under regular exam conditions* provides an unbiased, objective method to gauge their exam preparation, and also helps them target topics and problem types that gave them difficulties for targeted studying. Students who have come to the authors' offices in the past asking for help to do better on exams often state that they studied by working out old exams. However, upon closer questioning, we often find that they did not work the exam under normal exam conditions (timed, with only a calculator and an equation sheet, if allowed). Working out old exam problems casually with resources (course notes, web) and then looking up the answer to each problem immediately after working it out gives students a false sense of "knowing."

To get a realistic assessment of their knowledge and an accurate feel for the upcoming exam, students need to take practice exams under the same conditions as the real exam, and then grade the exam after taking it. Students can then skip the topics/problem types they got correct and focus on the topics/problem types they got wrong for further study. As they are figuring out how to work out a problem that they got wrong on a practice test, it is important to stress to students that they need to identify/verbalize what exactly caused the difficulty: Was it a conceptual error, and if so, what was it and how can it be avoided in the future? Was it a procedural error? Was it applying the wrong concept to the problem's context, and if so, what are the contexts under which that concept applies and does not apply? These types of questions force students to reflect on their learning and add desirable difficulties to their exam preparation.

- **Implement effective learning practices in organizing courses.** In preparing homework assignments and midterm exams in our courses, try to incorporate interleaved practice by having some cumulative problems in assignments and tests throughout the entire course. This serves several purposes: To convey to students that physics knowledge is cumulative and inter-related; to keep students' knowledge in the course current; and to convey to students that to learn physics well one has to see both the big picture as well as how concepts and procedures build on each other and are related to one another. In addition, interleaving some isomorphic worked examples within homework assignments would help students who are stuck identify the nature of their difficulty and allow them to make progress. Since asking/answering deep questions is also an effective learning strategy, and since it is difficult for students to pose deep questions on their own because their knowledge and perspective are not well developed, provide students with deep questions they can pose for themselves during study sessions. For example, using a modified form of the strategy writing activity discussed in Chapter 3, suggest to students that, after solving a problem, they should ask themselves to name the major principle/concept they applied, the reason why it applied to that context, and to state in words the procedure used to apply the principle/concept; this high level task can also be required for some subset of homework problems. As discussed earlier, questions such as these are difficult for students to answer and thus engender useful reflection on problem solving practices.

- **Help students improve their judgments of learning by using objective measures.** As discussed in the research reviewed above, students, especially poorly performing students, are likely to base their judgments of how well prepared they are for an exam on familiarity with the subject matter rather than on competence with the subject matter. Attempting to remedy this problem is exacerbated by the fact that poorly performing students think they performed above average even after taking an exam. This disconnect from reality is not amenable to quick fixes. One recommendation we would offer is for instructors to construct and have available a short 4–5 problem representative "mini-test" of an upcoming test and offer it as a diagnostic tool to students (in our office or at a predetermined place/time) using realistic exam conditions. Have students predict how many questions they expect to get correct prior to taking the mini-test, and immediately following. Then grade the mini-test and observe possible discrepancies between students pre- and post-predictions and the actual grade on the mini-test. We are likely to find the same result as in the previously reviewed research—students who perform poorly in the mini-test will have predicted that they would do above average in both of their predictions. Showing underperforming students first-hand that their predictions about their current state of knowing are inaccurate, and that they behave the same as students nationwide, opens the opportunity for a dialog on how to curb bad study habits and how to obtain more objective measures of preparation. We should keep in mind that students are very hesitant to abandon study methods that work in other courses since they will view it as risky behavior, and in addition, they do not know what study habits to adopt instead. However, seeing that what they are doing is not helping them succeed in the course allows instructors to offer concrete suggestions for adopting more effective study strategies.

References

Ackerman, R. & Zalmanov, H. (2012). The persistence of the fluency-confidence association in problem solving. *Psychonomic Bulletin & Review*, **19**, 1187–1192. doi: 10.3758/s13423-012-0305-z

Ambrose, S.A., Lovett, M., Bridges, M.W., DiPietro, M. & Norman, M.K. (2010). *How Learning Works: Seven Research-Based Principles for Smart Teaching*. San Francisco, CA: Jossey-Bass.

Ariel, R., Dunlosky, J. & Bailey, H. (2009). Agenda-based regulation of study-time allocation: When agendas override item-based monitoring. *Journal of Experimental Psychology: General*, **138**, 432–447. doi: 10.1037/a0015928

Benjamin, A.S., Bjork, R.A. & Schwartz, B.L. (1998). The mismeasure of memory: When retrieval fluency is misleading as a metacognitive index. *Journal of Experimental Psychology: General*, **127**, 55–68. doi: 10.1037/0096-3445.127.1.55

Bjork, R.A. (1994). Memory and metamemory considerations in the training of human beings. In J. Metcalfe and A. Shimamura (Eds.), *Metacognition: Knowing about Knowing*, pp. 185–205. Cambridge, MA: MIT Press.

Bjork, E.L. & Bjork, R.A. (2014). Making things hard on yourself, but in a good way: Creating desirable difficulties to enhance learning. In M. A. Gernsbacher and J. Pomerantz (Eds.), *Psychology and the Real World: Essays Illustrating Fundamental Contributions to Society (2nd edition)*, pp. 59–68. New York: Worth.

Blasiman, R.N., Dunlosky, J. & Rawson, K.A. (2017). The what, how much, and when of study strategies: Comparing intended versus actual study behaviour. *Memory*, **25**, 784–792. doi: 10.1080/09658211.2016.1221974

Dunlosky, J., Rawson, K.A., Marsh, E.J., Nathan, M.J. & Willingham, D.T. (2013). Improving students' learning with effective learning techniques: Promising directions from cognitive and educational psychology. *Psychological Science in the Public Interest*, **14**, 4–58.

Dunlosky, J. & Thiede, K.W. (2013). Metamemory. In *The Oxford Handbook of Psychology*, edited by D. Reisberg, pp. 283–298. doi: 10.1093/oxfordhb/9780195376746.013.0019

Dunning, D., Johnson, K., Ehrlinger, J. & Kruger, J. (2003). Why people fail to recognize their own incompetence. *Current Directions in Psychological Science*, **12**, 83–86. doi: 10.1111/1467-8721.01235

Ebbinghaus, H. (1913). *Memory: A Contribution to Experimental Psychology*. New York: Columbia University.

Ehrlinger, J., Johnson, K., Banner, M., Dunning, D. & Kruger, J. (2008). Why the unskilled are unaware: Further explorations of (absent) self-insight among the incompetent. *Organizational Behavior and Human Decision Processes*, **105**, 98–121. doi: 10.1016/j.obhdp.2007.05.002

Franklin, S.V., Sayre, E.C. & Clark, J.W. (2014). Traditionally taught students learn; actively engaged students remember. *American Journal of Physics*, **82**(8), 798–801. https://doi.org/10.1119/1.4890508

Griffin, T.D., Jee, B.D. & Wiley, J. (2009). The effects of domain knowledge on metacomprehension accuracy. *Memory & Cognition*, **37**, 1001–1013. doi: 10.1037/0003-066X.59.1.29

Händel, M. & Dresel, M. (2018). Confidence in performance judgment accuracy: The unskilled and unaware effect revisited. *Metacognition and Learning*, **13**, 265–285. doi: 10.1007/s11409-018-9185-6

Händel, M. & Fritzsche, E.S. (2016). Unskilled but subjectively aware: metacognitive monitoring ability and respective awareness in low-performing students. *Memory & Cognition*, **44**, 229–241. doi: 10.3758/s13421-015-0552-0

Heckler, A.F. & Sayre, E.C. (2010). What happens between pre- and post-tests: Multiple measures of student understanding during an introductory physics course. *American Journal of Physics*, **78**(7), 768–777. https://doi.org/10.1119/1.3384261

Hiebert, J. & Grouws, D.A. (2007). The effect of classroom mathematics teaching on students' learning. In Lester, F.K. (Ed.) *Second Handbook of Research on Mathematics Teaching and Learnin*, pp. 317–404. Information Age Publishing Inc.

Kelemen, W.L., Winningham, R.G. & Weaver, C.A. III. (2007). Repeated testing sessions and scholastic aptitude in college students' metacognitive accuracy. *European Journal of Cognitive Psychology*, **19**, 689–717. doi: 10.1080/09541440701326170

Koriat, A. & Ma'ayan, H. (2005). The effects of encoding fluency and retrieval fluency on judgments of learning. *Journal of Memory and Language*, **52**, 478-492. doi: 10.1016/j.jml.2005.01.001

Kornell, N. & Son, L.K. (2009) Learners' choices and beliefs about self-testing. *Memory*, **17**, 493–501. doi: 10.1080/09658210902832915

Kruger, J. & Dunning, D. (1999). Unskilled and unaware of it: How difficulties in recognizing one's own incompetence lead to inflated self-assessments. *Journal of Personality and Social Psychology*, **77**, 1121–1134. doi: 10.1037/0022-3514.77.6.1121

Mestre, J.P. (Ed.) (2005). *Transfer of Learning from a Modern Multidisciplinary Perspective* (393 pages). Greenwich, CT: Information Age Publishing.

Mestre, J.P. (2002). Probing adults' conceptual understanding and transfer of learning via problem posing. *Journal of Applied Developmental Psychology*, **23**, 9–50.

Metcalfe, J. & Kornell, N. (2005). A region of proximal learning model of study time allocation. *Journal of Memory and Language*, **52**, 463–477. doi: 10.1016/j.jml.2004.12.001

Miller, T.M. & Geraci, L. (2011a). Unskilled but aware: Reinterpreting overconfidence in low-performing students. *Journal of Experimental Psychology: Learning, Memory, and Cognition*, **37**, 502–506. doi: 10.1037/a0021802

Miller, T.M. & Geraci, L. (2011b). Training metacognition in the classroom: The influence of incentives and feedback on exam predictions. *Metacognition and Learning*, **6**, 303–314. doi: 10.1007/s11409-011-9083-7

Mitchell, T. (1997). *Machine Learning*. New York: McGraw Hill.

Morphew, J.W. (2019). *Metacognitive Calibration in Introductory Physics Courses: Predictors and Interventions* (Doctoral dissertation). University of Illinois at Urbana-Champaign, Champaign, IL.

Newell, A. & Rosenbloom, P.S. (1981). Mechanisms of skill acquisition and the law of practice. In J.R. (Ed.) *Cognitive Skills and Their Acquisition*, pp. 1–55. Hillsdale, NJ: Lawrence Erlbaum Associates.

Pashler, H., Bain, P.M., Bottge, B.A., Graesser, A., Koedinger, K., McDaniel, M. & Metcalfe, J. (2007). Organizing Instruction and Study to Improve Student Learning (52 pp). US Department of Education report, NCER 2007-2004.

Rebello, N.S. (2012). How accurately can students estimate their performance on an exam and how does this relate to their actual performance on the exam? In N.S. Rebello, P.V. Engelhardt & C. Singh (Eds.), *AIP Conference Proceedings*, Vol. 1413, pp. 315–318. AIP. doi: 10.1063/1.3680058

Sayre, E.C., Franklin, S.V., Dyrnek, S., Clark, J. & Sun, Y. (2012). Learning, retention, and forgetting of Newton's third law throughout university physics. *Physical Review Special Topics – Physics Education Research*, **8**(010116). http://dx.doi.org/10.1103/PhysRevSTPER.8.010116

Sayre, E.C. & Heckler, A.F. (2009). Peaks and decays of student knowledge in an introductory E&M course. *Physical Review Special Topics – Physics Education Research*, **5**(013101), 1–5. https://journals.aps.org/prper/abstract/10.1103/PhysRevSTPER.5.013101

Scaife, T. & Heckler, A. (2011). Interference between electric and magnetic concepts in introductory physics. *Physical Review Special Topics Physics Education Research*, **7**(010104). http://dx.doi.org/10.1103/PhysRevSTPER.7.010104

Schlosser, T., Dunning, D., Johnson, K.L. & Kruger, J. (2013). How unaware are the unskilled? Empirical tests of the "signal extraction" counter-explanation for the Dunning-Kruger effect in self-evaluation of performance. *Journal of Economic Psychology*, **39**, 85–100. doi: 10.1016/j.joep.2013.07.004

Schmidt, R.A. & Bjork, R.A. (1992). New conceptualizations of practice: Common principles in three paradigms suggest new concepts for training. *Psychological Science*, **3**, 207–218. doi: 10.1111/j.1467-9280.1992.tb00029.x

Schneider, W. (2002). Memory development in childhood. In U. Goswami (Ed.), *Blackwell Handbook of Childhood Cognitive Development*, pp. 236–256. Malden, MA: Blackwell.

Shake, M.C. & Shulley, L.J. (2014). Differences between functional and subjective overconfidence in postdiction judgments of test performance. *Electronic Journal of Research in Educational Psychology*, **12**, 263–282. doi: 10.14204/ejrep.33.14005

Sinkavich, F.J. (1995). Performance and metamemory: Do students know what they don't know? *Journal of Instructional Psychology*, **22**(1), 77–87.

Sweller, J. & Cooper, G.A. (1985). The use of worked examples as a substitute for problem solving in learning algebra. *Cognition and Instruction*, **2**, 59–89.

Ward, M. & Sweller, J. (1990). Structuring effective worked examples. *Cognition and Instruction*, **7**, 1–39.

Wenzel, K. & Reinhard, M-A. (2019). Relatively unintelligent individuals do not benefit from intentionally hindered learning: The role of desirable difficulties. *Intelligence*, **77**, 101405. doi: 10.1016/j.intell.2019.101405

Chapter

7 Testing in the Service of Learning: The Testing Effect and How it Promotes Long-Term Retention

7.1. What does research on the "testing effect" tell us?

In Chapter 6 we discussed effective and ineffective learning strategies. It turns out that testing is an effective learning strategy for long-term retention of information. Because testing is typically not used by students and faculty as a learning method, and because of an abundance of recent research pointing to the usefulness of testing for learning, we devote this short chapter to testing as a learning tool. Testing is often considered a dirty word among both students and faculty. Non-physics majors fear physics tests likely more than tests in other subjects. Generating several multiple-choice tests in large introductory courses is not among the favorite activity of faculty given how time-consuming it is, and open-response tests may be easier to make up but time-consuming to grade. The types of tests alluded to in the previous sentences are *summative* tests intended to evaluate students' knowledge to assign grades. Another type of testing, called *formative assessment*, is not used to generate grades but rather to help shape instruction to maximize student learning (use of clicker questions in large classes, as discussed in previous chapters, is an example of formative assessment). Over the last two decades, an increasing number of studies from the learning sciences indicate that testing (of the formative type) helps students retain their learning over longer periods of time—an effect called the *testing effect*.

7.1.1. What is the testing effect?

The testing effect can be summarized as follows (Dunlosky *et al.*, 2013; Pashler *et al.*, 2007; Roediger & Kapricke, 2006): When comparing studying material to being tested on the material, those spending their time being tested (after an initial study period) show greater long-term retention of the material than those spending an equal amount of time just studying the material. The effect is robust—perhaps most surprising, the testing effect holds even when performance on the tests is lack luster and even if no feedback is given on performance immediately following the tests. The qualifier "long-term retention" is crucial in the previous description. As the research reviewed below will demonstrate, repeated studying of material yields better performance on summative tests administered *immediately following* the study compared to equivalent time spent on testing; however, when tested one or more weeks later, the trend reverses, with those who spent relatively more time being tested significantly outperforming those who spent time in repeated studying. Perhaps this is why so many students rely on cramming as the preferred method of studying for high-stakes tests since it yields positive (but ephemeral) short-term payoffs. As instructors we want our students to retain the physics knowledge we teach them and testing is a tool we can use to promote long-term retention.

7.1.2. Experimental findings on the testing effect

A typical study of the testing effect by Karpicke and Roediger (2007) went as follows. Three groups of students were tasked to learn 40 unrelated words. During study, the words were presented on a screen at the rate of 3 seconds per word. During test, students were given 2 minutes (note that this is the same amount of time spent studying) to recall as many words as they could. The three groups were in the conditions STST, SSST and STTT, where S means a study trial and a T means a test trial (recalling as many words as possible). Each S or T trial was administered sequentially and words were randomized in each study trial. All three groups did the same four-trial set 5 times. Thus the experiment lasted approximately 40 minutes (plus a little "set-up" time between trials). Participants were tested immediately following each trial, and all participants returned after one week to take a final recall test. Results showed that the percentage of words recalled initially rose steeply across the first three four-trial sets and then reached an asymptote in the 78–88% range by the last set. The STST group did best with about 88% recall at the end of the fifth set, followed by the STTT group at about 81%, followed by the SSST group at about 78%. Thus all three conditions did about the same at final testing, but with a trend favoring testing. When tested one week later, the STST group did best with about 68% of the words recalled, followed by the STTT group at 63% with the SSST group recalling the fewest words at 55%. This is impressive given that the SSST groups had studied the list of words 15 total times versus only 5 times for the STTT group. Thus the group that engaged in the most study time did worst one week following the experiment; in other words, testing trials generated at least as much or more learning as did study trials. These types of studies have been reproduced by others with slightly varied conditions, all showing that long-term retention is better for groups that practice memory retrieval with testing rather than with studying. However, cramming (more study sessions compared to testing sessions) consistently wins out for tests conducted immediately following study.

A similar study by Wheeler, Ewers, and Buonanno (2003) also involving memorizing 40 unrelated words and comparing studying the list five times (SSSSS), versus one time with four back-to-back recall tests (STTTT) resulted in the typical cross-over pattern shown in Fig. 7.1. Studying the list five times has a large advantage if testing is done immediately after study, but one week later the single study followed by four recall tests condition does better. It is worth emphasizing that in the SSSSS condition participants were exposed to the entire list of 40 words five times, whereas in the STTTT condition participants were exposed to the 40 words only once and then re-exposed to only those

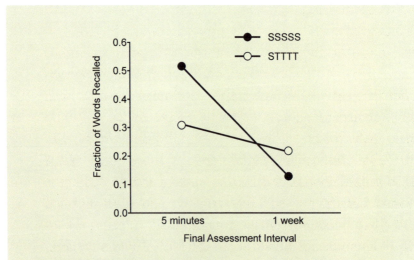

Fig. 7.1. Recall of 40 words after all study, or study followed by four tests after two different delay periods.

words they could be recalled during the four tests! Roediger and Karpicke (2006) describe these types of finding as follows:

> *Repeatedly studying material is beneficial for tests given soon after learning, but on delayed criterial tests with retention intervals measured in days or weeks, prior testing can produce greater performance than prior studying (pp. 189).*

Similar results have been obtained in studies using "paired associates," which are pairs of words to be learned. Word pairs take a variety of forms in different experiments; for example, English–English pairs such as chair-table or chair-horse, nonsense words paired with English words, and even Swahili–English pairs in some experiments.

7.1.3. Relevance of the testing effect for physics instruction

The attentive reader is likely now thinking, "How is this relevant to physics?" After all, conceptual learning and problem solving in physics is a whole lot more complicated than learning list of words. To be fair to lab-based cognitive psychology experiments, researchers choose tasks that can be learned in single 1–2 hour sessions to make experiments manageable. In order to conduct learning experiments in subject areas, especially one as complex as physics where learning takes considerable time, would require longitudinal studies that are much more difficult to conduct. Nevertheless, a smaller number of studies show similar findings when using more complex reading materials (see examples described in (Roediger & Karpicke, 2006)) and in classroom studies where learning conditions are difficult to control (McDaniel *et al.*, 2012; McDermott *et al.*, 2014). A recent study also demonstrated a testing effect within engineering disciplines (Morphew *et al.*, 2019).

As an example of a study that used more academically relevant materials, Roediger and Karpicke (2006b) had college participants read scientific passages in two experiments. In one experiment two groups were compared where one group studied the passages twice (Study–Study) and one group studied the passages once and then in a free-recall test wrote down all the main ideas they recalled from the passages (Study–Test). Three additional testing sessions were held 5 minutes, two days or one week following learning during which participants again free-recalled what they could remember from the passages. Figure 7.2 shows the findings from the experiment. As in the word recall studies reviewed above, the Study–Study group had the advantage in the test administered 5 minutes after learning. However, two days and one week later, the pattern reversed, with the Study–Test group doing significantly better than the Study–Study group. A second experiment compared three different groups who read scientific passages, with group SSSS studying the passages in four successive periods, group SSST studying the passages for three successive periods followed by a recall test, and group STTT studying once followed by three successive free-recall testing periods. Final recall tests were then administered 5 minutes and one week later. Figure 7.3 shows the findings. It is striking how the SSSS group's ability to recall passage details dropped precipitously after one week, whereas the groups that were tested, although performing slightly lower that the SSSS group 5 minutes after learning, retained considerably more details one week later.

Another finding is worthy of mention in studies of learning that compared study to testing. When participants are asked to predict how well they would remember what they had studied, those in repeated study conditions thought they would

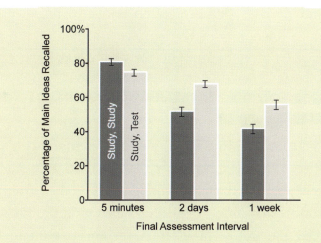

Fig. 7.2. Studying scientific text folowed test after varying delays.

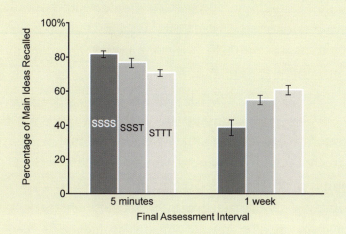

Fig. 7.3. Studying scientific text followed by free recall of main ideas after two different delays.

remember more than those in testing conditions (Dunlosky & Nelson, 1992; Roediger & Karpicke, 2006), perhaps due to their experience that cramming yields short term learning gains even though it is ineffective for long-term retention compared to testing; or perhaps this perception is due to repeated study yielding more fluency than testing (see Chapter 6). Thus, one cannot always trust one's intuitions for what works best.

7.1.4. Mechanisms leading to long-term retention from the testing effect

What mechanisms lead to better long-term retention with a combination of study and testing rather than just repeated studying? Several processes are likely at work. A hint comes from additional findings that tests requiring generation/production of material (i.e., effortful retrieval from memory) result in larger testing effect gains than tests requiring only recognition of the material, as in multiple choice tests (see Roediger & Karpicke, 2006 and references therein). Thus it seems that more effortful learning strategies result in better long-term retention. By practicing retrieval of information from memory during testing, students engage in deep processing of the material and strengthen memory pathways to the information (Kornell *et al.*, 2009). It is also thought that "test-potentiated learning," that is, benefiting from targeted study following a test, is another mechanism for the testing effect (Bjork & Storm, 2011; Wissman *et al.*, 2011). Interestingly, when provided with correctness feedback immediately following testing, testing effect learning gains have been found for items answered incorrectly during testing (Butler *et al.*, 2008; Richland *et al.*, 2008) as well as for related information that was untested (Carpenter *et al.*, 2012; Little *et al.*, 2012).

We have already discussed in Chapter 6 that popular yet ineffective learning strategies are those that provide students with a feeling of familiarity or fluency with the to-be-tested material. Repeated study is excellent for providing students with a feeling of fluency, but as discussed in Chapter 6, fluency with material does not imply competence with the material. From a student's standpoint, learning by repeated studying seems like a good choice—after all, it requires less effort and builds familiarity quickly. Testing oneself, in contrast, is effortful and generates less familiarity but (counterintuitively) results in better long-term retention of knowledge by building more connections/pathways to the information in memory. Test-enhanced learning fits Bjork's definition of a desirable difficulty discussed in Chapter 6, but it is a challenge to get students to adopt a "test yourself" strategy when studying, or to get instructors to use frequent testing as a learning strategy.

Many instructors make available to students old exams previously used in the course so that they may test themselves prior to taking the actual exam. Although this is an excellent idea, our experience is that students tend not to avail themselves of this opportunity (recall that taking tests is more effortful than re-studying material, and re-study generates more familiarity). Further, those students who do use old exams to prepare for an upcoming exam often use them inappropriately. In conversations we have had with students in our courses who lament they did not do well on an exam, we often ask them if they used the "practice tests" made available to them. Those students typically answer "yes" but when we probe more deeply how they used those practice tests they reveal that they used them casually and not under realistic exam scenarios. For example, they solve the problems with notes and textbook at their sides, and look up answers immediately after solving each problem. This does not measure performance under pressure in real exam circumstances; however, it builds familiarity with the material that is interpreted by students as competence with the material.

7.2. What are the implications of the testing effect for instruction?

We offer the following implications of the research reviewed above for instruction:

- **Formative assessments (i.e., assessments in the service of learning) are a powerful tool both for learning and for retaining what is learned.** Formative assessments afford several positive influences on learning. First, there is no pressure to do well on formative assessments so students can focus on evaluating what they know and don't know. Further, students actively participate in retrieving and using knowledge, thereby building and reinforcing retrieval links to the knowledge in memory. Formative assessments also makes students' thinking visible to the instructor, allowing instructors to spend relatively more time helping students grasp difficult ideas, moving them closer to coaches of learning rather than dispensers of information.
- **Tests that require generation/production of knowledge stored in memory promote lasting learning more than tests that only require recognition.** Tests that require generation of material require significantly more effort than those requiring only recognition. The added effort is a way of injecting desirable difficulties into the learning process, as discussed in Chapter 6. Students are likely to resist the expenditure of effort in learning in favor of easier but less effective learning approaches, such as studying and re-studying, which largely build familiarity with the material rather than competence with the material.
- **Combining testing with other successful learning strategies (as discussed in Chapter 6) would enhance the testing effect.** For example, when using formative assessment in a

course the instructor could test both the material currently being taught as well as previous material, thus combining testing with interleaved practice (as opposed to blocked practice).

7.3. Examples of teaching interventions based on learning research

Research on the impact of the testing effect on long-term retention of learning suggests a number of study and instructional strategies.

- **Communicate with students the powerful impact of the testing effect.** Since the testing effect is counter-intuitive, communicating to students the value of testing over repeated studying is valuable. Students will find it hard to believe that intensive studying is not as effective for learning and long term retention compared to a combination of studying and testing, but providing them with research findings will likely help them incorporate testing in their learning strategies.
- **Assess students' ability to link concepts to conditions for applicability.** Problem solving is crucial in physics and solving problems consists of applying concepts and procedures. However, before applying a concept, experienced problem solvers evaluate whether or not a concept is applicable to the specific situation under consideration; this type of knowledge is often referred to as "tacit knowledge" since experts use it without overtly making such knowledge visible during problem solving. Students in introductory courses often do not know when concepts can be applied to situations. Therefore, a very useful type of assessment that requires "deep processing"

is to provide students with a concept and ask them to state the conditions under which the concept can be applied, as well as conditions under which it cannot be applied (since this is a common error they commit). For example, Newton's second law is applicable to find the acceleration of an object when the net force on the object is constant; an object sliding down a frictionless curved ramp is not easily solved with Newton's Second Law due to the changing nature of the net force; conservation of mechanical energy can be applied only in cases where non-conservative forces do no work. One way to structure an assessment is to have a small group of students work collaboratively on analyzing a problem and determining whether or not a particular concept can be applied, and the underlying reason. A subsequent class-wide discussion would bring to light this type of tacit knowledge. Another activity that has been previously discussed that would also link concepts to conditions of applicability is strategy writing. The first two elements of strategy writing consist of identifying the concept(s) that applies to a problem and stating why the particular concept(s) applies to that specific situation, so one could shorten the strategy writing activity to one where problems are considered in view of the concept that could be applied to solve it and the reason for why it applies.

- **Use assessments that help students identify their own misconceptions.** Knowing that certain problems tempt students to apply incorrect intuitive notions, we can use those types of problems to refine students' understanding. One example is to give the problem below and ask students to generate a short series of procedural steps needed to solve it.

First note that this assessment requires students to recall and apply important physics ideas from memory. This assessment would also help identify many students' erroneous belief that the tension in the string is equal to mg. The intent here is to help students realize that application of physics concepts and procedures, in this case applying Newton's Second Law to both masses individually yielding the equations T = Ma and T – mg = –ma, is the appropriate approach which *should* make obvious that the tension is not mg. Since it has also been observed by physics education researchers that students can often write down correct procedures yet have underlying misconceptions, even if students write down the correct equations, the instructor can ask "Explain why the tension in the string is, or is not, equal to mg," hopefully leading to the obvious answer that if the tension were mg, the net force on m would be 0 and the mass would just hang there without moving. At some point later in the course, instructors could check to see if students are less likely to resort to incorrect intuitions by revisiting these situations under an Atwood Machine scenario.

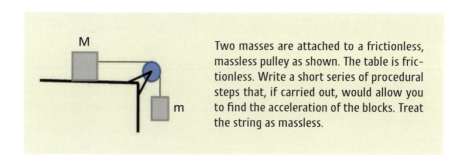

Two masses are attached to a frictionless, massless pulley as shown. The table is frictionless. Write a short series of procedural steps that, if carried out, would allow you to find the acceleration of the blocks. Treat the string as massless.

- Provide students with previous tests administered in your courses for them to practice on. This was a bullet listed in the previous chapter but it is worth repeating here.

It is important to ask students to take old practice tests under normal exam circumstances since the impression created by taking an old exam casually is that it is easier than the real test (as students so often tell us, despite the fact that exam averages remain fairly uniform year after year). Again, students tend to take the easier approach to exam preparation, namely studying and re-studying since this approach requires less effort and builds familiarity with the material. One analogy we like to use with students is to tell them that one does not train to run a marathon by watching videos of other people running marathons. Taking practice tests will let students know the actual state of their preparation so they can then take steps to remedy gaps in knowledge (making use of test-potentiated learning), as opposed to studying material they already know well.

References

Bjork, E.L. & Storm, B.C. (2011). Retrieval experience as a modifier of future encoding: Another test effect. *Journal of Experimental Psychology: Learning, Memory, and Cognition*, **37**, 1113–1124.

Butler, A.C., Karpicke, J.D. & Roediger, H.L. (2008). Correcting a metacognitive error: Feedback increases retention of low-confidence correct response. *Journal of Experimental Psychology: Learning, Memory, and Cognition*, **34**, 918–928.

Carpenter, S.K., Cepeda, N.J., Rohrer, D., Kang, S.H.K. & Pashler, H. (2012). Using spacing to enhance diverse forms of learning: Review of recent research and implications for instruction. *Educational Psychology Review*, **24**, 369–378.

Dunlosky, J. & Nelson, T.O. (1992). Importance of the kind of cue for judgments of learning (JOL) and the delayed-JOL effect. *Memory & Cognition*, **20**, 374–380.

Dunlosky, J., Rawson, K.A., Marsh, E.J., Nathan, M.J. & Willingham, D.T. (2013). Improving students' learning with effective learning techniques: Promising directions from cognitive and educational psychology. *Psychological Science in the Public Interest*, **14**, 4–58.

Karpicke, J.D. & Roediger, H.L. (2007). Repeated retrieval during learning is the key to long-term retention. *Journal of Memory and Language*, **57**, 151–162.

Kornell, N., Hays, M.J. & Bjork, R.A. (2009). Unsuccessful retrieval attempts enhance subsequent learning. *Journal of Experimental Psychology: Learning, Memory, and Cognition*, **35**, 989–998.

Little, J.L., Bjork, E.L., Bjork, R.A. & Angello, G. (2012). Multiple-choice tests exonerated, at least of some charges: Fostering test-induced learning and avoiding test-induced forgetting. *Psychological Science*, **23**, 1337–1344.

McDaniel, M.A., Wildman, K.M. & Anderson, L.L. (2012). Using quizzes to enhance summative-assessment performance in a web-based class: An experimental study. *Journal of Applied Research in Memory and Cognition*, **1**, 18–26.

McDermott, K.B., Agarwal, P.K., D'Antonio, L., Roediger, H.L. & McDaniel, M.A. (2014). Both multiple-choice and short-answer quizzes enhance later exam performance in middle and high school classes. *Journal of Experimental Psychology: Applied*, **20**, 3–21.

Morphew, J.W., Silva, M., Hermann, G. & West, M. (2019). Frequent mastery testing with second chance exams leads to enhanced student learning in undergraduate engineering. *Applied Cognitive Psychology*, **34**, 168–181. doi: 10.1002/acp.3605

Pashler, H., Bain, P.M., Bottge, B.A., Graesser, A., Koedinger, K., McDaniel, M. & Metcalfe, J. (2007). Organizing Instruction and Study to Improve Student Learning (52 pp). US Department of Education report, NCER 2007-2004.

Richland, L.E., Kao, L.S. & Kornell, N. (2008). Can successful tests enhance learning. In *Proceedings of the Twenty-Eighth Annual Conference of the*

Cognitive Science Society, p. 2338. Cognitive Science Society, Austin, TX.

Roediger, H.L. & Karpicke, J. (2006a). The Power of testing memory: Basic research and implications for educational practice. *Perspectives on Psychological Science*, **1**, 181–210.

Roediger, H.L., III & Karpicke, J.D. (2006b). Test enhanced learning: Taking memory tests improves long-term retention. *Psychological Science*, **17**, 249–255.

Wheeler, M.A., Ewers, M. & Buonanno, J.F. (2003). Different rates, of forgetting following study versus test trials. *Memory*, **11**, 571–580.

Wissman, K.T., Rawson, K.A. & Pyc, M.A. (2011). The interim test effect: Testing prior material can facilitate the learning of new material. *Psychonomic Bulletin & Review*, **18**, 1140–1147.

Chapter

8 Concluding Remarks

As you can tell from this book and the synthesis we wrote a few years ago (Docktor & Mestre, 2014), there is extensive research on the teaching and learning of physics from the Physics Education Research community as well as the learning sciences. Although some of this research is being used in the service of teaching and learning in physics classrooms, we still have a long way to go before EBIPs are more the norm than the exception.

We have highlighted key research findings about teaching and learning physics, however our review does not span the entirety of Physics Education Research. One area of emerging research in the field that we did not address is how non-cognitive aspects play a role in learning, such as motivation, expectations and beliefs about learning physics, mindset, stereotype threat, and self-efficacy. Many of these non-cognitive aspects of learning are also related to the under-representation of women and other minorities in STEM fields, particularly issues of self-efficacy and societal stereotypes and biases (for example, the notion that physics is for "brilliant men"). For those interested, a good place to start is the Physical Review focused collection on gender in physics: https://journals.aps.org/prper/collections/gender-in-physics. Hopefully in the coming years we will see advances in this area with concrete recommendations for instructors to promote a climate of diversity and inclusion in their classes.

We have focused on college-level intro physics, although many of the findings and teaching suggestions discussed can be used in high school physics and in upper-division college courses. In fact, there is also a research literature on teaching and learning in upper division physics (see the focused collection on PER in upper-division physics courses at https://journals.aps.org/prper/collections/upper-division-physics-courses).

Another important hole that needs to be filled is how to help our physics graduate students, who will become future professors, learn about the contents of this book. Since graduate courses for prospective physics Ph.D.s are virtually non-existent, the physics community found a "patch" remedy by having summer week-long programs for young faculty to learn about physics education teaching resources (see the Workshop for New Physics and Astronomy Faculty, https://www.aapt.org/Conferences/newfaculty/nfw.cfm). It is sad that immediately upon graduating with a Ph.D. in physics, young faculty need to be trained on EBIPs, as opposed to learning about EBIPs during the course of their graduate education.

It is also important to have a supportive structure in a physics department's administration to nurture and encourage faculty to use EBIPs in instruction. As we discussed in this book, many physics professors know about EBIPs and have even tried some in their teaching, but they often abandon EBIPs citing lack of support from the administration and time constraints. The STEM institution-wide response we discussed in Chapter 5 indicates the type of major accomplishments that can be achieved when teams of like-minded faculty work within a supportive administration. There is a story (whether or not it is apocryphal is unclear) of a department head coming to a young faculty member's lecture to observe him/her to provide feedback and to supply information to the faculty member's tenure portfolio, and upon finding that the instructor had broken students into small groups to work collaboratively, he yells back to the instructor "I'll come back some other time when you are teaching." Funny or not, it is also important to educate senior faculty and administrators on the value of EBIPs in instruction. Physical Review also has a focused collection of papers on preparing and supporting university physics educators: https://journals.aps.org/prper/collections/preparing-and-supporting-university-physics-educators

We hope you found the contents of this book useful and informative, and came away with a newfound excitement to try out a variety of instructional innovations in your own classroom!

Reference

Docktor, J.L. & Mestre, J.P. (2014). Synthesis of discipline-based education research in physics. *Physical Review Special Topics – Physics Education Research*, **10**(020119). https://doi.org/10.1103/PhysRevSTPER.10.020119

Index

A

abandoning intuitive notions   6
abstract and concrete representations   148
abstract concept   148
acceleration   14, 29, 30, 32, 180
accuracy of solutions   93
acquisition of knowledge   149
active learning   8, 25, 26, 111, 113, 114, 116, 118, 126, 128, 129, 151
active learning classes   126
active learning strategies   73, 111, 112, 115
activity-based physics   150, 151
adaptability   85
adopting physicists' ways of thinking   6
adoption strategies   127
advanced beginner   40
algebraic manipulations   65
algorithmic problem solving   113
alternate conceptions   14
amorphous memory store   76
analogy   64
analysis   38
analyzing problems   87
anchoring example   33
anchoring intuitions   33
angular impulse-angular momentum theorem   39
angular momentum   61, 71
animations   19, 21, 124
applying concepts   5, 143, 179
applying knowledge flexibly   115
apprentice   40, 91
appropriate understanding   24
asking/answering deep questions   157, 160
asking deep questions   147
assessing instruction   130
assessing problem solving skills   99
assessment in the service of learning   31
assessment of learning   113
assessments   8, 50, 63, 73, 75, 92, 95, 100, 130, 133, 150, 151, 160, 180, 181
assessments of student learning   4
attention   42
attitudes   102, 125, 133
authentic scientific practices   132

B

balls and tracks   17
balls-on-tracks   24
barriers to active learning   125
barriers to implementation   125
basic description   94
basic mathematical knowledge   85
basic physics concepts   33
beginning students   64
behaviorism   11, 12
beliefs   85, 102, 133
beliefs about learning   185
big idea   38
blank slates   13, 25
blocked practice   145, 153, 157, 179
brain dump   151
bridging analogies   33

C

carrying out investigations   132

carrying out the plan   93
categorization criteria   40
categorization tasks   88, 151
categorizing problems   51, 55, 66
change blindness   42, 46
checking calculations   85
checking the magnitude   86
chunking knowledge   84
class discussion   119
classroom demonstration   26
classroom instruction   7
classroom learning   149
classroom response systems   133
classroom spaces   122
class-wide discussions   180
clicker questions   131, 169
clickers   27, 29, 31, 128
clicker technologies   26
climate of diversity   185
coach   112
coaches of learning   178
coaching   69, 91, 92
cognition   112
cognitive apprenticeship   91
cognitive load   84
cognitive mechanisms   12
cognitive psychology   42, 141, 152
cognitive psychology experiments   173
collaborative activities   69, 124
collaborative groups   45, 89
collaborative problem solving   128
collect data   7
common-sense knowledge   17
communicate with students   179
communication tools   124
Communities of Practice (CoP)   127
competence   4, 40, 142, 153, 155–157, 161, 177, 178
compiling knowledge pieces   25
complex real-world problems   90
computer animations   17

computer-based tools   120
computer coaches   92, 104, 123
ConcepTests   116
concept formation   11, 22
concept inventories   26, 118, 151
concept mapping   31, 151
concept maps   75, 119
concepts   2, 5, 6, 8, 11, 33, 38, 39, 45, 62, 64, 65, 68, 69, 77, 84, 85, 88, 89, 100, 114, 116, 118, 119, 151, 159, 179, 181
concept scenario   89
concept(s)/principle(s)   66, 69
conceptual analysis   49
conceptual approach   83
conceptual development   8, 33, 65
conceptual difficulties   14, 15, 122
conceptual error   160
conceptual knowledge   25, 26, 66, 133
conceptual learning   173
conceptually challenging questions   131
conceptual questions   63, 117, 122, 124, 132
conceptual understanding   23, 25, 26, 73, 88, 117, 131
conceptual worksheets   122
concrete examples   148
conditions for applying concepts   180
conditions for applying principles   70
conditions of applicability   70
conducting investigations   130
conflict   13, 14, 30, 33
conflict management   132
conflict/resolution   15
connections   76
connections/pathways to memory   177
conservation laws   71
conservation of angular momentum   39
conservation of energy   21, 40, 43, 61

conservation of mechanical energy 22, 39, 70, 75, 148, 180
conservation of momentum 39
constructing appropriate understanding 25
constructing concepts 23, 24
constructing explanations 132
constructing knowledge 13, 24, 26, 111
constructivism 11, 13, 24
constructivist epistemology 112
constructivist learning theory 111
constructivist views of learning 11, 12
content coverage 76, 125
context 38
context-rich problems 88, 100, 103, 122
contextual experiences 23
contextual knowledge 23
control group 50, 51
cookbook-style 120
Cooperative Group Problem Solving 100, 122
coordinating knowledge 16
coordinating knowledge pieces 22
course grade 66
course management systems 115
cramming 144, 157, 158, 170, 172, 175
cultural shift 7
cumulative exams 145, 146

D

decline in memory 151
decline in performance 150
deeper processing 157
deeply rooted misconceptions 23
deep processing 176, 179
deep questions 147
deep structure 50, 66–68, 148
deep understanding 64
delayed testing 144, 173
demonstrations 119
departmental norms 125
departmental support 125
department chair 128
describe the physics 94
designing experiments 130
desirable difficulties 143, 146, 147, 157, 160, 177, 178
Devising a Plan 93
diagnostic assessments 99, 133
diagnostic tests 63, 130
diagnostic tool 161
disciplinary collaborations 129
disconnected facts 102
discussion section 69
discussion session 121
dispensers of information 178
distributed practice 144, 152, 153, 158
doing science 115
double curse 155

E

Educational Opportunity Program 63
educational psychology 141, 152
education faculty 129
education-related collaborations 129
effective learning practices 160
effective studying 158
effective study strategies 142, 157, 162
efficacy of reforms 128
effortful learning strategies 176
effortful retrieval 176
elaborate feedback condition 52
electric field 151
electric forces 77, 151
electricity and magnetism 150
electric potential 151
embedded mentors 128
energy 42, 150
engagement 23
engaging students 111
engineering courses 128
engineering departments 127
engineering disciplines 173
engineering majors 126

enhanced student learning 7
equal and opposite forces 14
equation-based approach 41
equation hunting 103
equation manipulation 70, 78, 100
equations 38, 41, 46, 65, 102
equilibrium 27, 28
eradicating misconceptions 14, 16
erroneous intuitions 5
erroneous notions 14
erroneous reasoning 16, 22
evaluate the answer 95
evaluating solutions 85
evaluation of classroom practices 7
evidence-based instructional practices (EBIPs) 3, 7, 83, 114, 125, 127, 130, 185–187
evidence-based reforms 127, 128
exam performance 125, 154
example problems 91
exam preparation 157, 159, 160, 182
exams 76, 92, 95, 104, 177
exam scores 126
exam wrapper 159
executed solution 56
execute the plan 94
expectations 85, 102, 185
experienced solvers 92
experiment 7
expertise 37, 39, 41, 64, 65
expert-like analyses 46, 51
expert-like approaches 85
expert-like behavior 46
expert-like computer tool 50, 51
expert-like problem solving 46
expert–novice differences 40
expert–novice research 8, 37, 46, 63
experts 3, 38–43, 45, 46, 50, 55, 64, 69–71, 77, 78, 83, 87
expert's blind spot 5, 64
experts' knowledge 64
expert's perspective 22, 64

exploring problems 87
exponential decay 150
exponential rise 149
eye movements 42
eye-tracking 42, 88

F

FACTs 119
fading 91
familiarity 4, 142, 153, 156, 157, 161, 177, 178, 182
feedback 91, 92
feel good strategy 142
feeling of familiarity 176
financial resources 131
finding errors 88
flipped classrooms 124, 128
flow charts 75
fluency 153, 156, 176
focus the problem 94
force 13, 14, 33
Force and Motion Conceptual Evaluation 26
Force Concept Inventory 26
force diagram 95
force of gravity 14
force problems 77
forces 29, 30, 95, 150
force vectors 77
forgetting curve 150
formative 113
formative assessments 31, 113, 115, 116, 119, 132, 133, 169, 178
formative assessment techniques 112
formulating explanations 43
framework 102
free-body diagram 30, 87
free-recall testing 174
frequent testing 152, 177

G

gas laws 32

gauging exam preparation   159
gender in physics   185
general knowledge test   153
generation/production   176
generation/production of knowledge   178
geometric optics   32
grading   99
grading structure   76
graduate courses   186
graduate education   186
greater performance   173
group activity   69
group work   121
growth mindset   144

H

hands-on activities   122
heavy objects fall faster   6, 13, 16, 24, 112
hierarchical analysis tool   47
hierarchical flow chart   75, 76
hierarchical representation of concepts   62
hierarchical structure of physics   75
hierarchy   75
hierarchy of physics   76
high-ability students   143
higher retention   76
highlighting   8, 142, 156
highlighting/underlining text   142
high-performers   155
high school physics   186
high-stakes tests   170
holistic problem solving   83
homework   4, 65, 69, 92, 104, 141
homework assignments   32, 56
homework solutions   92
How People Learn   130
how students learn   4
human behavior   11
hunches   6

hunting for equations   45

I

identifying principles   70
illusion of understanding   130
immediate feedback   150
impetus   15
implement EBIPs   4
implications of research on problem solving   100
important physics ideas   61
improved communication   93
impulse-momentum theorem   39
in-class practices   65
incompetent individuals   155
incorrect analysis   50
incorrect intuitions   181
incorrect intuitive notions   180
individual accountability   132
ineffective learning strategies   176
ineffective study techniques   142
initiate   40
innovative teaching strategies   75
institutional barriers   131
instructional activities   33
instructional implications   2
instructional reforms   130
instructional strategies   32
instructional suggestions   65
instructional techniques   142
instructor guidance   131
integrated classrooms   123
integrated lab-lecture classroom   122
intelligent tutors   104
interactive engagement   114
Interactive Lecture Demonstrations   32, 118, 119, 131
interactive pre-lectures   124
interference   151
interleaved practice   145, 146, 153, 157, 160, 179
internal decisions   152

interpreting data   132
interventions   65
introductory course   127
intuitions   6, 176
Investigative Science Learning Environment (ISLE)   120
isomorphic worked examples   147, 160

J

jeopardy problems   88, 89, 103
journeyman   40
judging   85
judgments about learning   141, 154
judgments about realistic motion   17
judgments of learning (JOL)   154, 156–158, 161
justifications   77
justifying principles   56
justifying problem-solving decisions   77
Just-in-Time Teaching (JiTT)   116, 124

K

kinematics   39, 95
knee-jerk intuitions   31
knowledge   13
knowledge construction   13, 16, 23
knowledge in memory   178
knowledge in pieces   15, 17, 22, 24
knowledge organization   37, 115
knowledge organization in memory   39
knowledge pieces   16, 17, 21, 24
KWL chart   119

L

laboratory activities   130
laboratory experiences   120, 122
laboratory experiments   132
lack of facilities   131
lack of support   131, 186

lack of time   125
lasting learning   143, 178
learning   13, 112, 113, 152, 156, 173, 174, 178, 179
learning and forgetting curves   150
learning curve   149
learning episodes   141
learning experiments   173
learning gains   126, 176
learning is not a spectator sport   129
learning research   65
learning sciences   170, 185
learning strategies   160, 169, 177
learning word lists   173
lecture-based instruction   112
lecture-based physics class   113
lecture demonstrations   32, 33
lecture method   23
lectures   3, 4, 62, 122
limiting cases   86
link maps   76
Logical Progression   99
logistic sigmoid function   149
longer-term interventions   55
longitudinal studies   173
long-term learning   84, 129
long-term retention   100, 130, 141, 151, 169, 170, 172, 175–177, 179
Looking Back   93
low-ability students   143
low-achieving students   76
low-performers   155
low-performing students   155

M

magnetic fields   151
major principles   47, 56, 62, 75
making predictions   14, 33
making students' thinking visible   113, 178
management systems   124
manipulating equations   83

map of concepts   76
massed practice   144, 153, 157
massed practice/cramming   152
master   40
mathematical complexity   87
Mathematical Procedures   99
means–ends analysis   41, 84
measured outcomes   126
mechanical energy   71
memorization   85
memory   38, 39, 65, 84, 148, 149, 176, 178, 181
memory load   41
memory pathways   176
memory retrieval   172
mental dialogue   86
mental resources   41
metacognition   85, 86, 112, 152
metacognitive judgments   153, 155
metacognitive monitoring   152, 154
metacognitive skills   85, 104
metacognitive strategies   113, 115
microscopic model   33
midterm exam   57
mindset   185
mind wipe   151
mini-test   161
Minnesota Assessment of Problem Solving (MAPS)   99
minority students   63
miscalibration   158
misconceptions   6, 8, 14–17, 22–26, 29, 32, 33, 73, 74, 112, 114, 133, 153, 180
misinterpreting concepts   23
misinterpreting implications   22
mixed ability groups   132
model appropriate behaviors   104
modeling   70, 77, 91
modeling expectations   92
model of learning   149
momentum   61, 71, 150

monitoring problem solving processes   85
motion diagram   95
motivating students   70
motivation   85, 185
multi-concept problems   62
multiple-choice exams   69
multiple-choice questions   26, 27, 116
multiple-choice tests   169, 176
multiple contexts   115, 142
multiple representations   122

N

naive theories   14
negative reaction   125
negative reinforcement   12
neophytes   3
net force   180
network   102
new concept   23
Newton's Laws   32
Newton's laws of motion   77
Newton's Second Law   27–30, 39, 40, 148, 180, 181
Newton's Third Law   6, 14, 150
Newton's three laws   61
non-cognitive aspects of learning   185
non-conservative forces   70
nonsense syllables   149
novices   5, 37–43, 45, 46, 50, 55, 64, 76–78, 84, 87, 91, 147, 148
novices' categorization criteria   51
nuanced understanding   23
number crunching   93

O

objective judgments   157
objective measures of learning   158
objective measures of preparation   162
objects fall at the same rate   13, 16
online homework   104, 123, 150

online homework systems   92
open-response tests   169
optimizing learning   141
organizational skills   145
organizing physics knowledge   65
out-of-class experience   123
overcoming misconceptions   15
overconfidence   155
overextending implications   22
Overview   95
Overview, Case Study Physics   62

P

pattern matching   38, 84
patterns of forgetting   149
patterns of learning   149
pedagogical expertise   127
peer discussions   131
Peer Instruction   116–118, 126, 131
peer learning   132
peer reflections   86
peer reviewed publications   129
perceptions   126, 156
perceptions of learning   8, 141
performance under pressure   177
personalized tutoring   123
perspective   38
PhET   121
physical representation   95
physical situations   119
physical world   14, 24
Physics Approach   99
physics concepts   23
physics department's administration   186
Physics Education Research   114, 185
physics education teaching resources   186
physics graduate students   43, 186
physics-naive students   19, 21
physics principles   40, 44
physics reasoning   31, 88

physics scenario   147
physics students   19, 21, 22
Physlets   121
pictorial representation   95
planning   85
plan the solution   94
plug-and-chug   41, 84, 87
poorly performing students   157, 161
posing meaningful problems   147
positive feedback   76
positive interdependence   132
positive reinforcement   11
potential and kinetic energies   75
power law decay   150
power law function   149
practice exams   160
practice tests   154, 182
pre-class questions   124
preconceptions   14, 22, 62, 121
predictions   119
pre-lectures   118, 124
pre-post learning gains   151
pretests   32
principal investigators   128, 129
principle-based categorization   55
principle-based criteria   55
principle-based reasoning   55
principle identification   78
principle identification exercises   78
principles   39–41, 45, 50, 51, 61, 62, 65, 68, 69, 77, 84, 85, 88, 100, 151
principles in categorizing problems   51
prior knowledge   11, 111, 112
private "theories"   25
private understanding   14, 15, 22, 23
problem-based learning   89, 128
problem categorization   40, 51, 66, 69
problem categorization task   50, 57
problem decomposition   85
problem posing   88, 89, 103
problem representation   86

problem solutions   102, 122
problem solving   2, 5, 6, 8, 11, 41, 45, 62–64, 66, 69, 76, 83, 85, 91, 92, 100, 121–123, 132, 146, 173, 179
problem solving assessment   51
problem solving differences   45
problem solving difficulties   87
problem solving frameworks   91, 92, 102, 103
problem solving instruction   91
problem-solving procedures   159
problem solving process   87, 92
problem solving skills   99, 104, 124, 133
problem solving strategies   86
problem solving task   50
problems' surface attributes   55
procedural error   160
procedural knowledge   71
procedures   38, 41, 181
procedures for solving problems   56
productively struggling   126
productive problem solving behaviors   103
productive problem-solving skills   86
productive struggle   144
proficient   40
promoting expert-like behavior   46
proposals   129

Q

qualitative analyses   45, 84
qualitative observations   121
qualitative problems   62
qualitative questions   62
qualitative reasoning   114
qualitative understanding   131
quantitative experiments   121
quantitative problems   62
quantitative problem solving   118, 131
quizzes   92, 95, 104

R

ranking task exercises   103
ranking tasks   88, 89
reading comprehension   85
realistic motion   21
RealTime Physics (RTP)   121
real-world knowledge   85
real-world problems   88, 103
recall tests   172, 174
recitation   121
recitation experience   120
reconstructing knowledge   26
refining students' understanding   28, 124, 180
reflection on problem solving   161
reflective journal   124
reformed instruction   127
repeated studying   170, 174, 176, 177, 179
repetitive task   149
representation of problems   87
rereading   8, 142
re-reading notes   156
research   8
research-based instructional strategies (RBIS)   114, 119, 120, 125
research evidence   1, 156
research on learning   6
research on problem solving   83
research productivity   126
research university   128
restructuring physical space   123
re-studying   178, 182
re-studying material   177
retaining information   144
retaining knowledge   145
retention   84, 178
retrieval links   178
retrieval of information   176
retrieving and using knowledge   178
retrospective confidence judgments (RCJ)   154

reviewing course notes 158
reviewing notes 4
rewarding students 104
role of concepts in problem solving 65
role of concepts/principles in problem solving 65, 66
rolling balls 23
rubric 99, 100

S

scaffolding 71, 91, 92, 144, 152
schema 85
schema-driven strategies 85
science and engineering faculty 129
scientific concepts 14
scientific passages 174
scientific reasoning skills 133
scientific thinking 112
S-curve 149
search-based strategy 41
selecting appropriate concepts 99
selection of problems 103
self-efficacy 185
self-explanations 86, 104
senior faculty 187
sense making 6, 12–14, 114
shallow learning 143
short term learning 175
similarity-based approach 84
simulations 122
single-principle problems 71
slowing down 22
social network analyses 128
solving problems 38, 47, 65, 69, 70, 83, 119, 132, 143
spaced/distributed practice 157
spaced practice 144
sparse-feedback condition 52
Specific Application of Physics principles 99
speed 15, 21
speeding up 22
spread of innovations 128
STEM 2, 7, 185
STEM faculty 129
stereotype threat 185
strategizing a solution 66
strategy 56, 57, 69–71
strategy writing 56, 61, 69, 70, 77, 78, 93, 147, 161, 180
strategy writing class 61
strategy writing students 61
strong expectations 22
structural and cultural change 129
structural change 146
structural constraints 125
structured cooperative group work 132
structured laboratory experiences 132
student attitudes 125, 126
Student-Centered Active Learning for Undergraduate Programs (SCALE-UP) 123
student-centered instructional approaches 114
student perceptions 126
student resistance 131
students' attitudes 118
students' erroneous beliefs 181
students' memories 61
students' perception 126
student strategies 57
student–student discourse 114, 131
Studio classroom 122
studio format 115
study habits 8, 141, 142, 157, 158, 162
studying 141, 152, 156, 170, 172, 173, 178, 182
study sessions 154
study strategies 142, 156
study time 157
subjective judgments 157
summarizing 142, 156

summative tests 169, 170
supportive administration 186
surface attributes 41, 42, 50, 64, 66, 68, 78, 148
surface features 40, 67, 68, 84
surface similarities 40
survey data 128
synthesis problems 88, 89, 103, 151

T

tacit knowledge 5, 41, 64, 65, 67, 69, 70, 77, 78, 179, 180
taking tests 177
targeted studying 159
teaching and learning 2
teaching and learning of physics 185
teaching and learning practices 7
teaching by telling 23, 112, 129
teaching correct scientific concepts 14
teaching evaluations 4, 7
teaching examples 2
teaching generalizations 13
teaching interventions 25, 65, 102, 131, 158, 179
teaching practices 65
teach the way you do research 6, 7, 128
technology-enhanced resources 116
templates 92, 102
tension 29, 74
tenure portfolio 187
test-enhanced learning 177
testing 8, 169, 171–176, 179
testing effect 169–171, 173, 176, 178, 179
test-potentiated learning 176, 182
tests 141, 181
textbook presentations 124
textbooks 76
thematically-relevant 42
theoretical description 94
think aloud 21
think-pair-share 31, 116, 119

top-down approach 70
topics covered 118
traditional class 61
traditional laboratories 120, 130
traditional lectures 116, 118
transfer 100, 113, 141
transfer of learning 129, 130
transferring knowledge 145
treatment group 51
tutorials 122
Tutorials in Introductory Physics 32
tutorial workbook 122
tutoring systems 123
two-column solution 73, 94
two-principle problems 57, 71
type of institution 126

U

unbalanced force 29
under-confidence 155
underlining text 156
underlying conceptual structure 66
underlying physics 44
underperforming students 156, 158, 162
under-representation of women 185
Understanding the Problem 93
undesirable learning behaviors 123
University of Illinois 127
upper division physics 186
Useful Description 99
using models 132

V

variable names 55
vector 151
velocity 14, 32
video-based materials 124
visual cognition 42
visualizing problems 85

W

web-based homework   69
web-based pre-lectures   126
well-organized memory   64
what experts and novices notice   45
what experts notice   41
what novices notice   42
what, why and how of solving a problem   56
WISE strategy   93
word recall studies   174
work   70
work and energy   75
work collaboratively   73
work done by conservative and non-conservative forces   75
worked examples   146, 147
work-energy theorem   39, 61, 75
working collaboratively   127
working memory   84
worksheets   32
Workshop for New Physics and Astronomy Faculty   186
Workshop Physics   115, 121, 122
writing strategies   57

Y

young faculty   186

About the Authors

José P. Mestre is an emeritus Professor of Physics and Educational Psychology at the University of Illinois at Urbana-Champaign. Since earning his Ph.D. in theoretical nuclear physics, his research has focused on the learning of physics, making many pioneering contributions in areas such as the acquisition and use of knowledge by experts and novices, transfer of learning, and problem solving. He was among the first to publish scholarly articles on the use of classroom polling technologies (clickers) to promote active learning in large classes, and is a co-developer of Minds-On Physics, an activity-based high school physics curriculum that is heavily informed by learning research. Most recently, his research has focused on applications of methodologies common in cognitive science (e.g., eye-tracking) to study learning and information processing by physics novices and experts. He has served on many national committees and boards for organizations such as the National Research Council, The College Board and Educational Testing Service and the American Association of Physics Teachers, and has offered Congressional testimony on The Science of Learning. He has published numerous research and review articles on science learning and teaching, and has co-authored or co-edited 19 books. Mestre served as Associate Dean at the University of Massachusetts-Amherst in the College of Natural Sciences and Mathematics, and both as Chair of the Department of Educational Psychology and as Associate Dean for Research at the College of Education at the University of Illinois-Urbana/Champaign. He is a Fellow of the American Physical Society with citation: "For ground-breaking applications of principles and methodologies from cognitive science to physics education research and for elucidating expert-novice performance differences in physics learning and problem solving."

Jennifer L. Docktor is an Associate Professor of Physics at the University of Wisconsin – La Crosse. After completing a physics teacher preparation program at North Dakota State University she earned her M.S. in High Energy Physics and her Ph.D. in Physics Education Research at the University of Minnesota. Her doctoral research focused on the Development and Validation of a Physics Problem-Solving Assessment Rubric. She spent two years as a postdoctoral fellow in Cognitive Science at the Beckman Institute for Advanced Science and Technology at the University of Illinois at Urbana-Champaign as part of a unique interdisciplinary research group on physics learning and cognition. She has collaborated with José on a variety of projects including conceptual problem solving in high school physics, categorization, and using eye-tracking technology to study physics representations. In 2010, they co-authored a commissioned paper for the National Academies report on Discipline-Based Education Research which was later published in Physical Review as the article Synthesis of Discipline-Based Education Research in Physics. In addition to these endeavors she is involved in several national efforts surrounding physics teacher preparation including the Physics Teacher Education Coalition (PhysTEC) and the project Get the Facts Out about STEM Teacher Recruitment. She has served on national committees for the American Association of Physics Teachers and currently serves as editor-in-chief for the American Physical Society's Forum on Education newsletter.

Printed in Poland
by Amazon Fulfillment
Poland Sp. z o.o., Wrocław

26298395R00118